HELPING YOUTH IN CONFLICT

SUCCESSFUL PASTORAL COUNSELING SERIES

HELPING YOUTH IN CONFLICT

FRANCIS I. FRELLICK

PRENTICE-HALL, INC.   ENGLEWOOD CLIFFS, N.J.

Helping Youth in Conflict
by Francis I. Frellick

© 1965 by Prentice-Hall, Inc., Englewood Cliffs, New Jersey.

Library of Congress Catalog Card Number: 65–11884

Printed in the United States of America.

T 38683

PRENTICE-HALL INTERNATIONAL, INC., *London*

PRENTICE-HALL OF AUSTRALIA, PTY., LTD., *Sydney*

PRENTICE-HALL OF CANADA, LTD., *Toronto*

PRENTICE-HALL OF INDIA (PRIVATE) LTD., *New Delhi*

PRENTICE-HALL OF JAPAN, INC., *Tokyo*

To those who give themselves to
vital Christian ministries with
young persons in conflict

INTRODUCTION

This series of books represents the most comprehensive publishing effort ever made in the field of pastoral care. These books could not have been published twenty-five years ago or probably even ten, for the material was not then available. In the past, single books have been available covering different phases of the task. Now we are bringing the subjects together in a single series. Here we present a library of pastoral care covering the major topics and problems that most pastors will encounter in their ministry. Fortunately, not all of these problems need be faced every week or even every month. But, when they are, the minister wants help and he wants it immediately.

These books are prepared for the nonspecialized minister serving the local church, where he is the most accessible professional person in the community. It is a well-accepted fact that more people turn to clergy when in trouble than to all other professional people. Therefore, the pastor must not fail them.

Russell L. Dicks
General Editor

CONTENTS

FOREWORD

This book is the fruit of experiences such as those to which it invites its readers. In 1955 a series of related opportunities began drawing my interests to the field of the Church's ministry with delinquent and hard-to-reach young people. While preparing a dissertation on this theme, I became a group process observer for an experiment in group therapy at the Charles Hayden Goodwill Inn for Boys in Boston, Massachusetts. Simultaneously I was campus representative for Andover Newton Theological School in a project designed to discover new Christian ministries in a slum area of Boston largely deserted by churches.

The following year I was one of seven graduate students given the opportunity to participate in a federal pilot project aimed at developing methods for dealing effectively with delinquent young people. That work was with the Boston Juvenile Court and its Citizenship Training Group program, under the tutelage of the nearby Judge Baker Guidance Center, Inc.

During that period I was assigned by the Boston Children's Service Association to work with a small gang of delinquent boys in Somerville, Massachusetts.

Following this, I became associate minister at Immanuel Baptist Church in Portland, Maine. There came the opportunity to practice some of the things learned in the above experiences and in my four quarters of clinical pastoral training.

Four years later a call came to inaugurate a program in Evansville, Indiana, to help build the potential of lay Christians to more effectively minister to the needs of delinquent and emotionally disturbed young people. That project has continued as a major responsibility of the Evansville Council of Churches.

I cannot name the persons to whom I am most indebted in the writing of this book. They are the boys and girls from whose lives I have drawn the majority of my illustrations. My relationships with them have been of a confidential nature, and so I have renamed them here. They have been my teachers and I hope they may be yours through the medium of this book. I am much indebted to them.

There is one other grateful acknowledgment to be made. It is for the first-draft typing of the manuscript, the review of the text and the extra parental responsibility shouldered by my wife during the preparation of this book.

May the Lord shepherd us who seek in His name Christian ministries with young persons in the midst of conflict.

Francis I. Frellick

HELPING YOUTH
IN CONFLICT

CHAPTER ONE

THE JUVENILE

"Juvenile" is a dirty word to many people. It frequently refers to small children, as, for example when one speaks of "juvenile furniture." However, anything related to childhood is quite distasteful to many an adolescent person; that's something which he asserts he's left behind for good. (Actually most authorities agree that he is officially a child until he is eighteen years of age.) Yet you may hear him effectively squelch one of his peers with an icy, "Don't be so juvenile!" Large numbers of adults assume that "juvenile" means delinquent. "Juveniles" are overgrown, sex-crazed teenagers, according to them, who have no respect for authority, are completely amoral and are in fact only a step away from becoming full-fledged adult criminals. Small wonder, then that this label "juvenile" is often resented by those to whom it is applied! It should be common knowledge that in its social sense "juvenile" simply means young. Thus it follows just as simply that a juvenile delinquent is merely a young person found to be delinquent. This observation is not made facetiously; rather it is an initial reminder that juvenile delinquents and other youth in conflict are persons; . . . strangely, even embarrassingly, like ourselves.

Modern psychology and penology assert that a delinquent child should not be treated as an adult criminal. He is neither a criminal in the eyes of the law nor an adult. He needs help. So does the adult for that matter, but the needs of the young offender differ from those of his older counterpart.[1] (Failure to recognize this can seriously hamper any efforts to deal meaningfully with young people in trouble.) This is to say that concerned people ought to know some-

[1] Benjamin Fine, *1,000,000 Delinquents* (New York: World Publishing Company, 1955), p. 274.

thing about what it is to be a juvenile person. Yet how many times a day do we hear terms like "juvenile," "teen-ager," "child" and "adolescent" used interchangeably? Each has to do with varied and sometimes overlapping phases of the physiological, sociological and psychological development of young persons. Some knowledge of their particular meanings is essential to clear thinking and appropriate actions with a given boy or girl or groups of young people. Accordingly we shall shortly deal with the distinctive character of the phases of childhood development known as preadolescence or later childhood and adolescence.

Under the old Anglo-Saxon Law, the chief concern in all matters of delinquency was the responsibility of the offender. It was believed that said responsibility could be chronologically established. Thus, specific age limits came to be the major determinants of the punishability of a convicted offender. Although we are growing away from such easy procedures today, vestiges of them are still evident. Under the statutes of a majority of states today, a child may be adjudicated delinquent if he is over the age of seven years and under eighteen. He is a minor until he is twenty-one. The thirteenth century legal code in England held that an individual was not punishable for a crime unless he had reached the age of ten and one-half years. That age was thought to mark the beginning of the age-next-to-puberty and thus one's responsibility for his actions. This system was at times sadly unappreciative of individual exceptions and variations from the norm. It was further limited in its implicit assumption that punishment was appropriate for all "responsible" offenders, but that's another matter. Increasingly today it is being accepted that emotional maturity and responsibility can't be computed on a purely chronological basis.[2]

All of this nevertheless suggests a field upon which to focus the main concerns of this book. Clearly the consensus of the legal traditions just cited is that in general children come to a new degree of responsibility for their behavior at about that place in their lives which psychologists call the beginning of later childhood or preadolescence. This period and subsequent adolescence carry the young person through the remainder of his official childhood. They nicely

[2] Paul W. Tappan, *Juvenile Delinquency* (New York: McGraw-Hill Book Company, Inc., 1949), pp. 12–13.

cover the time during which one is commonly thought of as "a youth." In terms of age we're talking of a range from nine to twenty-one years. This affords a convenient springboard from which to begin. No springboard can be rigid, and neither should these initial limits be so if they are to be truly useful. They are descriptive and not definitive. Further, it will be necessary to look beyond them from time to time in order to more accurately appreciate them.

Finally, since the word "delinquency" has already come up several times we ought to have some common understanding of its use here. Delinquency is a legal term, and refers to "any act which might be brought before a court and adjudicated." Thus the only difference between a young person who is found to be a delinquent child, for example, and other youthful "bad-actors" is that the former has transgressed his first and greatest commandment: "Thou shalt not get caught!" Many acts of a delinquent nature go undetected or for other reasons are not referred to court. It is precisely because the young adjudicated delinquent is basically no different from other juveniles that we must now give considerable attention to the world and major problems of the young person. Let's begin with his later childhood, or preadolescence.

Preadolescence

The rates of growth and change which suddenly accelerate at this point and carry through adolescence are nothing short of phenomenal. They are second only to those which occur between the time of conception and the earliest days of a baby's life. Although a developing fetus gains size and weight at a fantastic rate during gestation and graduates at birth to an entirely different medium, what happens in the development with which we are now to be concerned is no less dramatic. Furthermore, the persons who enter upon this time of life do so with a much more complicated set of new tools, including, as we shall see, experiences which often affect their reactions.

There are some who say that preadolescence and adolescence ought really to be taken together under the latter heading. I hope it will be evident in what follows that there are sufficient differences in rate and qualities of change to make the separation worthwhile, at least for purposes of understanding. For that matter there are enough who look at the matter in this fashion to assure us of good company.

Roughly, in speaking of preadolescence we should be talking about that period of experience usually covered between the ages of nine and twelve. Its significance lies in the development of the individual rather than his age. This must not be forgotten, for, as will be noted, boys and girls may individually be clear exceptions to the rule. Thus chronological predictions of change must not be taken too seriously here of all places in human experience. The reader should keep in mind that we are fundamentally concerned with persons, not exhibits of "stages." If Jim's teachers or his parents deal with him in terms of the stage through which they think he should be passing at a given moment, they might be quite unable to be of any help at all. (He might not have reached that point yet, or he may have long since gone on to wrestle with "later" problems!) Not a few times I have talked with parents who were much concerned over the fact that their son or daughter had not yet become interested in heterosexual companionship. They had read or heard enough about when it was supposed to happen to be worried when their child failed to conform to the pattern. Since no parent rejoices at the possibility that his child may be "different," undue emphasis upon chronological norms can be dangerous. Parents suffer first in such predicaments and often subsequently so does the child who may have to sustain their anxious, though perhaps unwitting pressures. Keeping all this in mind, let us turn our attention to some of the more notable changes usually experienced by preadolescent boys and girls.

Physical Change. Following birth the high rate of bodily growth begins to taper off. By the time of preadolescence that rate has reached its lowest level so far. In a real sense, this is the lull before the storm. Right at this point we encounter a significant, general distinction between boys and girls. The latter usually come to this respite from growth first. Previously there has been little by which to distinguish boys from girls in their overall development. Now the girls tend to move ahead of the boys, sometimes by as much as two full years. The first evidence of change appears to be a resting of the body in preparation for subsequent puberty and adolescence. During this time of relatively slow growth both boys and girls seem to develop boundless sources of energy (much to the occasional dismay of distraught parents and teachers!). Mother may shake her head in bewilderment and sigh, "You never *used* to act up like this, Billy!" or Dad may be heard to observe, "I just don't see how Susie can keep going like that all day long. I couldn't stand it myself!" And he couldn't, either! One apparent reason for this vigor has to do with a child's use of his energy. When a major portion of it must be expended in bodily growth, a smaller amount is thus available for activity. Conversely, if a boy or girl for a time nearly ceases to grow physically, his body economy can shift in the direction of greater activity. This idea seems further validated in the growth spurt which follows the resting period we have been discussing.

Almost overnight the tables are turned. The child whose failure to grow and fill out may have threatened parent and child alike begins to outgrow clothes faster than parents can pay for them. This new acceleration reaches its peak at the time of puberty, and from that point begins to slowly decelerate until the close of adolescence, when it comes about to an end. The body frame has usually reached its full development by the end of adolescence, although weight and its distribution may change thereafter: Thus it is that in the fourth and fifth grades in school girls are noticeably taller and heavier than boys. Furthermore, those who are, tend to be a little less exuberant and active than the boys and other girls they have preceded in their development. These general changes and sexual disparities have a real bearing upon the kinds of experiences encountered by church teachers and leaders of "Junior" or "Upper Junior" children. The girls' lead in body size and weight lasts only a short time. However, they move on to other sorts of change still ahead of the boys, particularly in terms of sexual maturation.

Primary Sexual Development.   While this sudden resumption of body growth is taking place, changes of other sorts are on the horizon. Many of them have to do with approaching sexual maturity, and these can be divided between primary and secondary characteristics. Both are evidence of the growing influence of the endocrine glands, especially the pituitary and the male and female sex glands or gonads. It is these glands which pour into the bloodstream the chemical substances which precipitate the sexual changes in puberty.

Primary sexual development in both boys and girls has to do with the readiness of the reproductive systems for procreation. At the point of puberty a girl's ovaries and uterus, or womb, will become capable of conceiving and nurturing a child. She will be physically capable of becoming a mother. Eventually, about every twenty-eight days she will enter into a cycle which begins with ovulation, includes the migration of a ripe ovum to the uterus, the preparation of the uterus for possible pregnancy, and, when this does not occur, the sloughing off the prepared uterine lining of blood, tissue and mucous through the vagina to the outside of the body. The first such menstrual flow is known as the menarche. It can be a very embarrassing or even frightening experience for the girl to whom this very natural process has not been adequately explained. This experience is still referred to by some as "the curse," the "female sickness," or is ominously referred to in many widely read publications as "those days."

With boys there is a parallel but later and different process by which the body approaches sexual maturity. The male reproductive system, the penis, the pouch (scrotum) which holds the testicles, and several minor internal organs, also matures under the influence of the endocrine glands. As a boy approaches puberty, both the testicles and the penis increase in size. This is because the male sex organs must not only be able to produce sperm cells but to transmit them to the upper end of the female vagina. At puberty and thereafter, barring the release of tension through either masturbation or coitus, the accumulating seminal fluid will occasionally demand and achieve release. This is normally accomplished by the emission of excess semen in what are known as "wet dreams." This, too, can be an unnerving experience for one who is unprepared. The combination of such an act with the obviously increased size of a boy's penis and testicles at puberty can be the cause of much anxiety, especially if he either leads or follows most of his peers in the latter development.

Secondary Sexual Development. So far we have only touched on the primary aspects of the sexual development which one approaches in later preadolescence. Actually, with few exceptions, the secondary changes which begin at this time are more obvious. Therefore, they may at times draw more attention and concern than the more basic changes already described. Here, too, the girl maintains her lead in the race of change. Usually the first of these secondary changes is the enlargement of the breasts. This obvious modification of her figure leads to a new focus of attention upon appearance. This can be a positive sort of thing if preparation by parents, and mother in particular, has helped her to view this as a natural process and one which will enhance her attractiveness as a young woman. Mother's help with this special concern in the selection of clothing can be a quiet and comforting assurance at this time. If Sally has been one of the last of her group to develop in this way, the change, when it comes, may be most welcome in spite of a lack of preparation at home. Mary, on the other hand may come unprepared to this situation ahead of all her peers. Now added to her developing menstrual cycle is the matter of her combined height, size and breast enlargement, all of which frankly make her stand out like the proverbial sore thumb. She may go to some extremes to try to hide the change, affecting bulky clothing and a slouched posture. Hiding these developments for most girls becomes increasingly difficult. There is also at this time a noticeable widening of the hips. These modifications of physique are actually the means by which the body becomes capable of sustaining pregnancy and giving birth to children. A further modification of physical appearance is occasioned by growth of hair on most of the body, especially in the pubic (genital) and axillary (armpit) areas. Brief blouses and short skirts often prompt girls to hide or somehow remove unwanted hair from the legs and underarms. Of the various procedures possible few are harmful, but each such measure should have the approval of one's physician.[3] This is true of all efforts to artificially modify the physical appearance, including the eventual selection of supportive and foundation clothing.

Where boys are concerned some parallel secondary changes are about to be observed. For example, there is a common tendency toward some swelling of the breasts. This is not nearly so marked as that of the girls, and is usually of short duration. Nevertheless it is frequently enough, even for the boy who has been somewhat prepared for it, to cause worry and shyness. The shower room at school can become a dreaded place during such time. Furthermore, with both boys and girls this swelling may be uneven, a little painful and often includes the temporary appearance of small "knots" or lumps

[3] Arthur Roth, M.D., *The Teen-Age Years.* (Garden City, New York: Doubleday & Company, Inc., 1960), p. 120.

within the breast. Fears of being a freak or of cancer may cause considerable anxiety at this point, and the discovery of the normality of such things can be reassuring if not entirely convincing.

New hair also appears on the boy's body in the same general areas as with girls, and, a bit later, also on the boy's face. An enlargement of the larynx, most noticeable in boys, is the reason their voices begin, in preadolescence, to "play tricks on them." Gradually Johnny's voice deepens, though in speaking it seems to jump back and forth from the old range to the new. Everybody smiles knowingly at the strange sounds he sometimes makes, but Johnny wishes they'd turn their attention elsewhere.

Generally speaking, a distinctive change in muscular development and weight distribution begins to become evident in boys at this time. Partly this is due to the growing emphasis placed upon more strenuous exercise for boys and the popular appeal of the manly physique. On the other hand, authorities on the matter feel that the inclusion of muscular development of the shoulders and legs is a part of the secondary sexual changes which take place in boys. The combination of these new peer-group values and the apparent natural tendency toward enlargement of the shoulder and leg muscles usually offers the promise of considerable prestige to the boy who develops a "good build." However, such an achievement is the product of a sort of discipline which is difficult for many a juvenile person.

Body Strangeness. These secondary physiological changes associated with approaching sexual maturity constitute together a new kind of challenge for the remainder of this period and on through adolescence. Briefly, it is the need to get acquainted with and use effectively the new body in which the preadolescent person finds himself housed.[4] Seemingly overnight the mirror becomes the *sine qua non* of personal grooming. Sis becomes terribly interested in clothes. From time to time she experiments in numerous ways to find acceptable ways to show off her developing figure. She and her friends include in their private talks more and more topics related to the changes taking place in them. Their smutty stories and nervous giggling over things with sexual overtones are all part of their efforts to discover just what sort of creatures they are coming to be. A

[4] Irene M. Josselyn, M.D., *The Adolescent and His World* (New York: Family Service Association of America, 1955), p. 19.

beautiful illustration of this process of exploration, discovery and wonder is to be found in the now-classic *Diary of Anne Frank*. Two paragraphs are here especially appropriate:

> I think what is happening to me is so wonderful, and not only what can be seen on my body but all that is taking place inside. I never discuss myself or any of these things with anybody; that is why I have to talk to myself about them.

> Each time I have a period . . . and that has only been three times . . . I have the feeling that in spite of all the pain, unpleasantness and nastiness, I have a sweet secret, and that is why, although it is nothing but a nuisance to me in a way, I always long for the time that I shall feel that secret within me again.[5]

The diary was kept while Anne's family was in hiding. Anne could find no real confidant in that tiny circle and so turned instead to her "Kit" (the diary) for such "talks."

The Search for Reality.   This search for the "real me" is not only a physiological quest. The preadolescent young person in the midst of so much change within and about himself comes naturally to a need for knowing "what's for *real*." Thus reality testing now becomes part of his approach to most situations. There develops a sort of rational censorship . . . a growing away from the world of romantic dreams and fancy out of which he is emerging. Reasoning supplants easy, unquestioning acceptance. He sees persons more objectively. He is sometimes disappointed and disillusioned about what he now sees, too. Thus the idolized college senior who lives in the neighborhood may appear in a vastly different light to the preadolescent boy or girl than was true the previous summer. Perhaps something of the sort occurs with respect to parents. It is not unlikely that one now turns increasingly toward his peers to establish models by which to pattern his behavior. As we shall see in the fourth chapter, that is part of what lies behind the formation of gangs among preadolescent young people. This is often appropriately called the "gang" age. This reality testing may be quite threatening to adults, especially if it is not accepted for what it really is. Incidentally, if what we as churchmen offer the preadolescent in the name of Christ cannot bear this sort of

[5] From *Anne Frank: The Diary of a Young Girl*. Copyright 1952 by Otto H. Frank. Reprinted by permission of Doubleday & Company, Inc. and Vallentine, Mitchell & Co., Ltd., London.

scrutiny, it ought not to be offered! Reality testing is not always the personal affront it is easily assumed to be. Rather, it may be an honest effort to objectify and test. That sort of effort is a major key to the development of a rational, strong faith. Within manageable limits it ought to be encouraged.

An increasingly significant factor in the search for reality is skill in reading. Failure to exercise and improve this capacity can be a real deterrent to achievement in school and social status as well. Reading continues to be the foundation upon which nearly every formal educative experience is built. It is the vicarious step beyond direct experience which can greatly extend the process of reality testing.

Interestingly enough, the Missouri (show me!) approach isn't used as frequently in the realm of social relationships. Here there still persists the tendency to deal with other persons in an unreasoned manner. The older child has not yet begun to take the "long look" at time either. Cohen states that a major characteristic of the gang subculture is its short-run hedonism.[6] The problem is even more evident in delinquent behavior as we shall find later. This is probably why the preadolescent boy or girl tends to turn to his or her peers for new values rather than to parents. If their focus is indeed that of the moment at hand, the planning for the future urged by adults would certainly appear inappropriate many times . . . very *un*realistic!

Nevertheless, the growing ability of the older child to put things together and take them apart rationally provides him with a growing degree of control over himself and the world about him. That in turn increases his appetite for independence. It's obvious from a number of observations that Eddie's parents don't know anything. They're beginning to have trouble with his math and science homework. He can do for himself more and more of the things for which he used to depend on them. They defend some of their stuffy ideas with everything but reason. And so, he concludes, "Who needs 'em?"

The Role of the Developmental Changes. We could continue to list other changes in the life and personality of the preadolescent which are not wholly physical, sexual, or intellectual. There are those who will say that there are other important areas of change to be considered in preadolescence. Blair and Burton, for

[6] Albert K. Cohen, *Delinquent Boys* (Glencoe, Illinois: Free Press of Glencoe, Inc., 1955), p. 30.

example, stress the adjustment of the individual to his social situation as the key to the discovery of the characteristics of later childhood.[7] They also include a reference in support of this position from the findings of a committee on Human Development at the University of Chicago. That committee lists in a position of comparatively minor importance the developmental tasks of accepting and adjusting to a changing body, approaching sexual maturity and maturing intellectual powers. This may be partly due to that committee's concern with children just a bit younger than those with whom we have been concerned. However, this writer is convinced that a recognition and an appreciation of these areas of change is indispensable to any adequate appreciation of the problems of both the preadolescent and the adolescent. There seems to be real evidence that these changes play roles of varying but considerable importance in most of the major problems which beset the preadolescent and the adolescent. This is not to say that they are causally related to all of these problems. More nearly they appear to "set the stage," as it were, for expression of the problems which come to the surface in these two periods of life. To borrow an analogy from chemistry, physical and sexual and mental changes arising toward the end of later childhood and continuing through most of adolescence act as catalytic agents, bringing about the expression of underlying problems which may have long lain dormant. A catalyst, in the language of chemistry, is a substance which increases the rate of a reaction without itself being changed. To a large degree this is the case with the changes we have been describing. However, there are instances where these changes may be themselves somewhat hindered or altered, as for example in the matter of emotional obstacles to the further development of reading skills previously mentioned. Thus the analogy breaks down at this point. Nevertheless it has served its purpose. Consider the following quotations from Hurlock on this matter of the importance of physiological, sexual and mental change and development in later childhood and adolescence:

> The physical changes and maturation of the sex apparatus that occur during the early part of adolescence exercise a profound influ-

7 Arthur Witt Blair and William H. Burton, *Growth and Development of the Preadolescent* (New York: Appleton-Century-Crofts, 1951), p. 180.

ence on the psychological changes which take place at this time. For that reason, what may appear to be proportionally too much space is devoted to a discussion of these physiological changes. . . . The author feels justified in this and attempts to prove the correctness of this approach by presenting evidence to show the close relationship between the physiological and the psychological aspects of development.[8]

Early books on adolescence gave little attention to the physical development of the adolescent. The reason for this was that there was limited knowledge of the relationship between physical, mental, emotional and social development. Only recently have the effects of physical growth on other aspects of development been understood and appreciated. Now it is a recognized fact that, as is true of the child, the physical development of the adolescent plays an important role in his concept of himself as an individual. . . . Psychology is not concerned with the growth of the body as such, but only insofar as it . . . has an influence on the behavior or mental ability of the individual.[9]

And then note this excerpt from a later portion of the same book:

There are a number of common causes which give rise to feelings of insecurity and uncertainty on the part of the adolescent and which, as a result, predispose him to be heightened emotionally. Not one of these is physiological in origin. . . . For that reason one can safely conclude that heightened emotionality during adolescence is attributable to social factors, not glandular, as was formerly believed to be true.[10]

Though the last of these quotations may appear to contradict the first two, this is not actually the case. Rather it clarifies the author's position and that of this writer. On the one hand Dr. Hurlock is speaking of the *influence* of physical, sexual and mental developments upon the psychological maturation of the individual who is preparing for or already is going through puberty and adolescence. Physical and/or sexual development, with the possible exception of some deformities, is seldom a true *cause* of juvenile problems. They may, however, and often do intensify underlying problems and frequently provide the occasion for the development of behavioral symptoms of maladjustment to those real dilemmas. The real problems of the preadolescent and the adolescent are not new developments,

[8] Elizabeth B. Hurlock, *Adolescent Development* (New York: McGraw-Hill Book Company, Inc., 1949), pp. vii–viii.

[9] *Ibid.*, p. 65.

[10] *Ibid.*, p. 118.

totally unrelated to what has gone before. Rather, both the older child and the adolescent are encountering anew the problems of their childhood or infancy, but in a new context of life which gives them more urgency than ever before. Wattenberg has this to say:

> Before he enters his teen years, each boy and girl already has a well-formed personality. To a large extent this influences the course of his later development. . . . What a youngster was like establishes as a point of departure for the path he takes as a teen-ager. Each . . . has his own set of strengths and weaknesses, his own problems and conflicts, his own ways of seeing himself and the world. Accordingly, for every one the experiences to come in his second decade of life carry different meanings, pose different obstacles, and open different avenues for growth. . . . Indeed, the unsettling effects of some of the events in his teen years may bring surprising developments which hark back to events of early childhood. . . . The evidence for the above conclusions is largely clinical.[11]

The first characteristics of the period of preadolescence listed by Blair and Burton concern the social attitudes and behavior of the preadolescent, and involve the rejection of adult standards, sex differentiation, and attachments to members of the same age level and sex. Is it not natural that these changes occur, if we consider the basic changes the child is experiencing at this period just before adolescence? This is a time, as we have already noted, when the child ardently seeks a more realistic understanding of himself and the world about him. He also gains new skills, better control of his body, greater manual dexterity, and, in general, an increased ability to manipulate things and even the people about him. He is gaining an increased awareness of the relationship of causes and effects. In short, he is gradually gathering to himself the knowledge, control and personal ability, both physical and mental, necessary to the more independent life of the adult. He craves freedom from the cramping restrictions and controls which have been placed upon him by persons and an entire adult social system which "knows better." For the child of this period, many of these adult controls under which he chafes are themselves very *un*realistic. He has not yet learned to take the long view of things, and thus the controls placed upon his total

11 William W. Wattenberg, *The Adolescent Years* (New York: Harcourt, Brace & Company, 1955), p. 41.

behavior seem to him to be groundless, and often merely the effort of adults to add to their own waning prestige. More and more the older child becomes convinced that he can actually entirely manage himself, and probably in a much more efficient and satisfying way than seems possible under an arbitrary regime of adult values to which he has so far been subjected. The inability to meet the demand of that adult code of life doesn't harmonize with the child's growing conviction of self-sufficiency. The appealing solution, and the one promising the most immediate appreciable results, appears to involve the emancipation from the controls of the adult world. As we shall see in the third chapter, this desire finds company and support in the associations of the play-group and the gang.

Add to this the fact already noted that girls in this period of development tend to mature physically about a year in advance of the boys, and the picture becomes more clear. Anyone who has worked with preadolescents has been aware of the very real dividing line which is drawn between the sexes at this stage in life. Almost exclusively, preadolescent young people seek members of their own sex as regular companions. This is definitely not a self-conscious effort to cover up an actual attraction to the opposite sex. The gap is real, and sometimes involves open hostility. A major reason for this separation is the advance of the girls into a new phase of life which introduces them to puberty almost a full year ahead of the boys. Here girls begin to adopt new values, seek the company of older children, give great attention to their appearance and to their relationships with the boys, and in general to enter into a stage of life where they are neither children nor adults. Boys, not yet having reached that later point in their parallel development, continue their rough boisterous pursuits and their gang associations, to the mixed puzzlement and exasperation of many a parent, and increasingly by those girls of the same age who have now stepped ahead. This is a difficult time for the boys. In one way or another they are frequently compared with these maturing girls and even scolded or severly punished for not behaving as they do. Thus faced with one degree or another of rejection from both the girls their own age and adults who want them to "grow up," the natural alternative is to turn exclusively to gang associations with other boys of the same age. Let the reader be assured that this sort of association is *not* necessarily a prelude to a life of crime. We will see in the fourth chapter what is the actual essence and appeal of the gang and what are some of its values.

For girls these changes about conclude participation in competitive, rough-and-tumble activities with the boys. They are encouraged to withdraw from these activities and to become more "lady-like." Clear distinctions begin to be drawn between boys' and girls' games. No longer can the boys count on including girls in such games as "Kick the Can," "Cops and Robbers," football or the like. Less and less are the girls interested in feats of strength or the ability to win fights. On the other hand, this will continue as a means to achieving status in the boys' gangs for some time.

For both the boy and girl at this time, the search for compatible associates has been narrowed down to a very select group. In a sense these combined periods of growth toward maturity are a veritable "no-man's land" for young people. Quite clearly the girls, and a bit later the boys, realize they are no longer children. Even before the changes directly connected with puberty, the superior strength, stamina and skills of the preadolescent set him apart from the younger children. Moreover, it seems to this writer to be an unwritten juvenile commandment that no young person, and particularly no boy shall select his friends from age groups much younger than himself. However, in situations where this is impossible to observe because of the absence of age peers, as perhaps in a small neighborhood where all the other children are younger, the desire for some sort of group experience may win out and draw the individual across the line. Certainly at this time there are no doorways by which to enter the adult world, and the very juvenile code mentioned above denies the preadolescent access to adolescent circles, for he could not even look the part. The only apparent solution appears to be that of turning more completely toward one sure source of acceptance and empathetic understanding, i.e., the group or gang of the same age and sex.

The deep need of the individual for that acceptance, his craving for affection and intimate relationships with others, the desperate struggle for status, and the search for an adequate means of self expression are by no means caused or even borne by the physical, sexual, or mental changes involved in later childhood, puberty or adolescence. These changes, however, do tend to make more urgent some sort of solution to these problems at this time.

So far, then, in this chapter we have treated the major physical, sexual and mental developmental changes of the period of pre-adolescence. We have stressed the point that differences between both the sexes and individuals make it impossible to predict exactly when this stage will begin for each individual. We have stated that this phase of growth usually begins somewhere within the age span of from nine to twelve years, with the girls about one year ahead of the boys at the start of this race toward maturity. Special attention was drawn to the importance of these major areas of development, *not* as *causes* of "juvenile problems," but rather as catalytic agents, increasing the rate and urgency of the individual's reactions to problems which actually reach far back into earlier childhood and even to infancy. Now let us look beyond, into that continuation of the process of maturation, which is said to begin with the somewhat elusive experience of puberty, and is called adolescence.

Adolescence

Perhaps this is one of the most misunderstood periods in a person's total development. It is frequently referred to as the "problem age," but the truth of the matter is that a large share of the problems connected with adolescence are those of *other* persons who have little or no knowledge about this tremendously important time of life but think they do. For them it therefore poses a real, though unrecognized difficulty.

Furthermore, recent rises in juvenile delinquency, the vast amount of popular fiction and movies depicting the asocial behavior of poorly adjusted adolescents, coupled with the much-publicized reports of rejections of youth from the armed services during the war due to evidence of mental and neurotic disorders—all these have tended to give many adults the impression that all adolescents are poorly adjusted and, to varying degrees, delinquent in character. This lack of understanding is not a new phenomenon, although for reasons we shall discuss shortly, the lengthened period of adolescent life is a bit more complicated today than ever before.

For a long time in history, this stage in the growth toward individual maturity was taken to be synonymous with what we now designate as puberty. That is to say, it was believed that there were two chief periods in the life of the individual: childhood, and adult life. Thus the child in the primitive tribe who had come to sexual maturity was ceremonially ushered into adulthood by means of rigorous rites of initiation and testing, and from that time on "put away forever childish things." Even today such practices are observed by remote tribes of semi-primitive people. In this framework maturity was simply sexual maturity—the point at which a boy or girl was capable of marrying and procreating children. Since the time when this was the commonly accepted practice, many things have changed, and most of these initiation rites have been outlawed. However, the sort of thinking which underlay them did not disappear as quickly, nor are its traces extinct today. Both the Greeks, especially the Spartans, and the Romans exerted much effort and the strictest discipline in training their boys to be capable warriors once they had reached the commonly accepted age of sexual maturity.

In the Middle Ages much the same condition was true in the life of the boy who had ambitions of one day becoming a knight. At fourteen years he became a squire, and from that time on trained himself, indeed lived, inasmuch as possible by the grand measure of knighthood. Much more recently, it was common in post-colonial days along the expanding frontiers of this country that children married and began new families almost as soon as they were sexually capable. Still later it became the custom, particularly in low-middle and lower class families to expect that a sexually mature child would assume adult responsibilities of living. For the boy this meant either the procurement of means to contribute to his "keep" at home, or self support away from home. For the girl, the physical signs of womanhood were also an indication that she was at last ready to be married. Thus her lessons in the art of housekeeping, the preparation of her trousseau, and the tested feminine strategies for attracting suitors were all intensified. By this time, however, the shifting from the role of a child to that of an adult had become a bit less sudden. The tendency had developed to think of the sexually mature child as *ready* for adult life, as represented by marriage, but this no longer amounted to an ultimatum to immediately make that change.

The Long Wait. Currently, especially in middle and upper class families, adolescence is generally considered to be of much greater duration, even as much as eight years. Legal age of maturity in the United States, in terms of voting power and responsibility for one's behavior is twenty-one. Elizabeth Hurlock in her excellent and comprehensive book *Adolescent Development* states: ". . . the more civilized a nation becomes, the longer is the transition from childhood to maturity and the more difficult it is to make this transition."[12] Today the adolescent must wait four, six or even eight years before he is accorded the recognition and privileges befitting an adult. Yet paradoxically, he is expected during this time to conduct himself in accordance with the social mores governing adult life. When he fails to do so he is punished for not behaving as an adult. Therefore in one respect the old concept of an abrupt transition from childhood to adult life is still in vogue, and the consequently widened chasm between expected behavior and recognized status is full of bewilderment and anxiety.

As yet we have none but adult norms by which to evaluate the pattern of living of the adolescent. Scientific studies of infancy and childhood have enabled us to recognize and even to predict basic trends in the total development of little children and thus to evaluate their reactions and general behavior. However, we have no such standards for the appropriate measurement of adolescent life patterns, save the established rules for adult conduct. We refuse to accord the adolescent the full privileges of adult life, but we have failed to provide him with standards befitting the "in-between" quality of the position to which we have thereby consigned him. Small wonder it is then that we call this the "Problem Age"! Mrs. Hurlock says that this tension is magnified by the lack of significant training of children to meet the demands of adult life. She admits the inclusion of vocational training and home economics courses in secondary school curricula, but insists that these programs do not offer much significant preparation for the sort of *maturity* later to be demanded, and often already expected of the adolescent. She feels therefore that the acquirement of manual skills does not amount to the type of preparation for adult life which seems to her to be most necessary. Indeed the general opinion appears at times to be summed up in words like these: "Oh well, don't lose hope; Johnny is just going through those 'problem times'; he'll grow out of it;—they all do." This seems to say

[12] Hurlock, *op. cit.*, p. 3.

further that there is little real need for the individual adolescent to do anything but wait for the "problems" to pass; after that he will be an adult. The trouble lies in the fact that the adolescent, of all people is probably least able to "just wait" until he finds he's become an adult. Let us review some of the reasons why this is so.

The Immediate Background of the Adolescent Situation. Adolescence is measured from the onset of puberty. We have already considered the early physical and sexual elements of change centering about puberty. The secondary characteristics of sexual maturity continue to develop for some time after the primary changes are established. Changes in voice, the new and increasing growth of body hair, and the almost universal problem of acne, are developments which commonly spread over the entire period of adolescence. These and the other changes already mentioned supply fertile soil for the development of many symptomatic problems. For example, adolescent life provides a sharp contrast to early preadolescence in terms of the available energy and vigor of the individual. He now tires easily and is far more susceptible to disease. The energy reserve of late childhood is greatly taxed by the demands of the pubescent growth spurt. Resistance of the youth is at a low ebb, though he may fail to recognize or accept the fact, in view of the very recent vigor of the period of his late childhood. In the same vein, a very disheartening discovery of the early adolescent is the fact that his control over his body doesn't develop at the same rate as his height and weight. This is the cause of most "adolescent" awkwardness. Boys may be especially alarmed to find that the skill and body control of late childhood seems to have been somehow lost. They spill things, trip over minor obstructions in their paths, and knock over all sorts of furniture and fragile things. Girls, now increasingly conscious of the appearance they make before others, especially the boys, are crestfallen over their awkward, gangling movements.

For the adolescent, personal appearance has become of great importance. Both boys and girls experience increasing attraction toward each other where a short while before there was clear rejection. Much attention is given to making a pleasing appearance before other adolescents, particularly those of the opposite sex. Problems are frequently involved at this point as well, for early adolescence is a period in which physical growth is frequently not uniform in rate or extent in all parts of the body. Blos speaks of this imbalance as the "asymmetrical growth pattern" of adolescence.[13] Considering the above factors of sudden growth, lagging controls and uneven rates of development of parts and systems of the body, to say nothing of the possibility of development which is sexually inappropriate, it is not strange that the adolescent attaches great importance to his outward appearance, and holds it to be of extreme importance not to deviate from the hypothetical norm—or to be notably "different" in any respect. Shaving is a case in point. Once his peers begin to shave, Jerry insists upon meticulously trimming all four hairs on *his* left cheek. This is proof positive that he is at last becoming a man.

For both boys and girls the physique is of great importance, but from different standpoints. Physical prowess in a boy is something worthy of the respect of both boys and girls. Thus activities which put a premium on speed, strength and agility are a gateway to popularity and group acceptance among both sexes. In some way most boys must satisfactorily demonstrate their virility before the group, and thus actually indicate their ability to protect themselves and, one day, a wife and family. Among the boys themselves, engagement in more virile sports activities and especially in fights is usually the primary key to acceptance in the group. Although our present economy currently puts a premium on scholastic achievement, the athletic individual can still be sure of acceptance and a certain degree of prestige.

Adolescent girls turn their attention to an attractive appearance. From the time of their first awareness that boys can be attractive, exciting persons, they begin to become increasingly conscious of their own personal appearance. The highest of premiums is placed upon good looks. The girl who is not blessed with a good figure or much facial beauty often feels somewhat handicapped. Nevertheless she learns that she can do much to enhance her appearance by the selection of attractive and tasteful clothes. She must keep abreast of the current styles and particularly the opinions on personal appearance among her own peer groups of girls and boys if she is to rate and date.

One common problem involving appearance of both boys and girls

[13] Peter Blos, *The Adolescent Personality* (New York: Appleton-Century-Crofts, 1941), pp. 231–232.

in adolescence is that caused by acne, a minor skin disturbance involving the malfunctioning of certain glands in the skin, which, because it usually affects the face, neck and shoulders, is often a major concern to appearance-conscious adolescents. This difficulty is most common in the earlier stages of adolescence.

The developments we have mentioned frequently have very significant psychological implications for the adolescent. The boy or the girl who experiences irregularities in the time or the extent of physical and sexual change sometimes is afraid of the reactions of his peers and therefore may seek unwholesome immature means of compensation. To refer again to the last-mentioned of these adolescent physical problems, a boy with particularly noticeable skin eruptions on his face may seek to escape associations with girls for fear of making a bad appearance and perhaps being rejected. He may decide the solution lies in the limitation of his relationships to his own sex as he did in his later childhood, and the adamant support of their philosophy that "girls are no d——— good!"

Stop, Look, and Listen!

There is an imminent danger at this point, and in view of the previous discussion, it ought to be clearly understood. For a long time there were people (and the species is in no immediate danger of extinction) who believed that the solution of the problem of delinquency as a whole must lie in the discovery and liquidation of that one thing which must be its universal progenitor. Friedlander writes:

> During the last century psychiatric research was inclined to maintain the existence of definite differences between the delinquent and the law-abiding citizen. At different times different theories were held as to the nature of the distinction, which was then considered to be the only factor in causing crime. According to the prevalent scientific trend of the moment, the shape of the skull and of the brain it enclosed, heredity, insanity, alcoholism, feeble-mindedness were each in turn for a decade or so considered to be responsible for producing criminals . . . a theory was framed first and afterwards applied to the criminal. . . . We know today that all those theories which ascribed the origin of criminal behavior to one single cause . . . were erroneous.[14]

[14] Kate Friedlander, *The Psycho-analytical Approach to Juvenile Delinquency* (London: Routledge & Kegan Paul Ltd., 1947), p. 5.

In the same manner we ought to be acutely aware of the danger in interpreting the preceding descriptions of the ideal physical, sexual and mental development patterns of maturation of later childhood and adolescence as being the key to an understanding of delinquency and the delinquent, or as the problems which, if properly met, will cease to "cause" delinquency. These changes and their irregularities *do not cause delinquency!* If that *were* true, it is very doubtful that there would ever be found a child who was *not* delinquent! The most damaging evidence against any theory naming one factor as the prime root of all delinquency is the cold fact that in a given situation two individuals, alike in nearly every respect, and facing an identical problem, frequently react *differently* toward it. Most slum children are *not* delinquents; nor are most poor children, city children, imbeciles or the physically handicapped. Most older children and adolescents, facing the sort of developmental experiences we have mentioned thus far, do not automatically become delinquent. Most of them fail to make adequate adjustment to some of those very dilemmas and yet only a very small minority are delinquent. It should be firmly fixed in our minds that the changes we have discussed are only factors which frequently intensify and make more urgent the solution of more fundamental problems. If this is true, it is high time that we turn our attention to those more fundamental problems, in order that we may grapple with essentials in the chapter on "The Delinquent Solution" to Juvenile Problems.

The Score So Far.   We've dug a footing and poured a foundation. Even before that we marked off the area of our operation. On the basis of legal tradition and psychological interpretations of personality development in children it seemed best for our purposes to apply the word "juvenile" to persons roughly between the ages of nine and twenty-one years. We ought not, however, to be so naive as to consider this as an exclusive focus for our concerns. It will be better if our efforts at illumination are more in the character of a floodlight, rather than a spot. We shall need again and again to remind ourselves that troubled persons are first of all *persons,* ever so much like "the rest of us." "Bad actors" perhaps, but always persons.

That is the point at which we began pouring the foundation. We have talked of two overlapping phases of development within the above-mentioned age range; preadolescence and adolescence. They lead to and from the experience of primary sexual maturation known as puberty. We watched the preadolescent child, seemingly suspended in his physical growth one moment, suddenly fairly exploding in a rush of body growth just as he comes up to puberty. We witnessed the sexual differentiation occasioned by the separate male and female timetables for this sort of change. We perused both the basic and the secondary sexual changes to be expected as one approaches and moves beyond puberty, noting how important the latter becomes to young men and women. It was pointed out that these changes in their individual combinations make it imperative that a young person be reacquainted with his strange new body structure and capabilities; i.e, "the new me." Coupled with these physical and sexual modifications, we found new patterns of thinking emerging. Significantly, the juvenile persons about whom we are here concerned begin at this time to crave a realistic approach to everything. He increasingly wants to be assured that anything he accepts is "for real." This even applies to himself, and the body strangeness to which we have just alluded.

Some time was then spent in assessing the role of the many accelerated changes which occur at this time in life. The fact the vast majority of juveniles successfully adjust to the many challenges of late childhood and adolescence discredits the thesis that developmental trends are the determinants of such problems as juvenile delinquency and emotional disturbance. Rather, it seems that said changes are more in the character of catalytic agents, facilitating reactions without becoming much further involved otherwise. The majority of "adolescent problems" are actually manifestations of problems with which the adolescents concerned have been wrestling through childhood. More will be said of those problems later. Suffice it to reiterate that the changes of this period plus new social attitudes and pressures make the more urgent some kind of resolution of the problems with which the adolescent has previously dealt.

In a real sense our discussion of adolescence implied that this is essentially a time of basic adjustment to the new body, social patterns and thinking processes associated with pubertal developments. This period of life is of longer duration than its predecessor. Moreover, we found that our society is further lengthening the period of waiting until one achieves acceptance as an adult.

Now we are ready to begin fashioning a more specific understanding of those troubled young persons to whose welfare this book is dedicated. We shall first try to appreciate some of the dynamics which upset the emotional applecart of some juveniles. Later, we'll address ourselves to the delinquent answer to these challenges, especially in the context of the gang. From then on we shall become engrossed in the fabrication of meaningful ministries for Christ with such persons. So—let's get with it!

CHAPTER TWO

FLIES In The OINTMENT

So we find our juvenile friend groping about in a veritable no-man's land between childhood and adult life. He is yearning to escape into a grown-up world. Yet no one will accept him there. He hasn't mastered the new tools and weapons with which he's been equipped. He's still a kid. And who of us would choose to take that long demanding journey again? Everyone "understands" his problems and everyone has an oversupply of advice for him. They know; they were teenagers once. Beneficently, they pass on a few tips, which, if practiced, are guaranteed to straighten him out. Then they turn away, leaving him alone again.

This is the plight of juveniles taken as a whole. Our announced concern, though, is with youth in conflict; the relatively tiny proportion of those who elect to fight it out with the world or any equally formidable adversary, or within themselves. What happens in an occasional young person that throws him into a continual scrap against persons, property and institutions? Why frequently does such action appear in only one child of a given family? Are there clues which will further extend our awareness of the real needs of these embattled young persons? How truly significant are those first five years of a child's life?

Socialization Assignments

Perhaps one fruitful way to come at the questions just raised is in terms of a review of the sort of relationships one is expected to find with others in his early life. We might call these basic socialization assignments. The first social task given each of us is the establishment of our own identity. In a real sense this is a life-time project (in fact all of these assignments share that quality). The solutions depend pretty largely upon the way others relate toward us; the place they give us in their lives. From the beginning, the feelings and actions of others make it increasingly clear to an infant just where he stands in his tiny world. He needs to be loved just as surely as he must be fed. In most instances, babies are wanted and loved to the point where they naturally conclude that they are the very center of their respective microcosms. All they have to do is give voice to their dissatisfactions and people come running from all directions, grandmother in the lead. The very physical health of the infant is partly dependent upon having an important place in his mother's life. One of the advantages of nursing a baby is the opportunity thus afforded for an intimate exchange of cuddling and loving gestures. In a strange world it is essential to know that one is lovable and in fact loved. Long before he can verbalize the feeling, a baby who is genuinely loved is gaining a satisfying understanding of who he is. That image will be the corner-stone upon which his personality will rest. As we shall see in a later chapter, Christians above all have good reason for helping to reveal the lovable nature of persons. It is enough now to stress the importance of being loved by others, and first of all, Mother.

Not all babies have this sort of help in their efforts to discover who they are. For them perhaps the message doesn't quite get through. If the mother frequently is upset and tense when she handles her baby it is that tenseness which is most likely to be communicated to the infant. Clinical studies have shown a clear relationship between the incidence of colic in nursing infants and the existence of emotional tensions in the mothers at feeding time. Communication in these early days, though non-verbal, is nevertheless clear. The same thing is true in the less intimate relationship of the baby with other persons in the family. All these relationships can be affected by factors over which the child has no control. For example, perhaps Ralph's conception was the precipitator of a "shotgun wedding." When that marriage flounders, he may become in his parents' eyes the very cause of their unhappiness. Susan may represent an unwelcome addition to an already intolerable financial situation in her family. If Alice has never accepted her husband as he really is; if in fact she now rejects him, she may tend either to reject or draw away to herself their children. In the one instance she may be heard to say things like: "Oh John, put that down! You're just as (*unacceptable quality*) as your father!" Or, on the other hand she may confide to her mother, "I'm so glad the children are more like me."

In some marriages misunderstanding and bickering take on the proportions of a floating prize fight. This writer vividly recalls several months' association with a confused, bitter, frightened and frightening boy who for fifteen long years had been only a spectator at a continuing battle between his parents. They had never really known he was around! Notice the factor which is common to all these regrettable situations: the problems of the parents took precedence over their relationship to their children. This sort of outside interference can and frequently does minimize and distort otherwise meaningful relationships. This is to say that the assignment of establishing one's identity may receive a severe setback when parents' expressions of love are stifled by their own problems. A really well nourished baby is well loved. One can in fact starve for want of love as well as the lack of food. The loved child has been given a definite place in his world. He doesn't have to try and manufacture one. He's not alone nor is he afraid. In short, he's ready to face his second social assignment, i.e., relating positively and successfully with the family about him.

Before long it begins to dawn on Junior that this is not exclusively his world. At times others seem to claim part of it for themselves. Mother begins making demands upon him. Among other far-fetched things she wants him to stay clean! Even good old Grandma takes Mother's side sometimes. For some reason Daddy insists that he's *not* to kick his baby brother until the little fellow drops what Junior wants for himself. At this juncture a wise strategy usually begins to develop in Junior's mind. Since those who make the rules at home are much larger than he, it becomes increasingly clear that it's usually best to swim with the tide when there's a difference of opinion. No longer can his own immediate pleasure be the sole determinant of his behavior. What happens later, when the size differential is gone will depend on the relationship which has undergirded the decisions along the way. If that has been a matter of size alone, Junior may be saying to himself, "Just wait until I'm big enough. . . ." A great deal depends at this point on how the needed controls and supervision are administered by the parents. These responsibilities must be executed in love, though at times all parents find this is easier said than done.

Children are born into a world which to them seems like a wonderland to make Alice's adventures by contrast quite commonplace. As they push buttons and turn knobs all sorts of marvelous things happen as if by magic. They accept this and enter with gusto upon exploratory adventures into this exciting world. One of the natural parts of that process is finding the outer limits within which they must operate. Thus the child is constantly probing and testing. At home this means finding just where his parents' control and supervision take precedence over his exploration, and, how this is accomplished. There may arise numerous occasions in the course of a child's waking day when it seems necessary to his parents to set some limits on behavior. Yet that very responsibility is one which requires a fine balance between protective control and healthy original inquiry; a balance, by the way, which migrates imperceptibly from the vicinity of the former toward the latter as the child (and the parents?) mature. Before this awful responsibility we who are parents often tremble. The fact that we can and do make mistakes in that effort without entirely ruining our children is a somewhat comforting discovery. It further implies that perhaps it is not so much a specific limit but the fact that a limit is set and how it is set that is of importance. For the better part of a year I had a detached assignment with a gang of teenage boys, all of whom had been found at least once to be delinquent. They had to find out at the beginning just where the limits were for their actions. A backward look at early experience with the boys makes it quite clear that the setting of limits on their behavior in a given situation has a calming effect on the group, in spite of their momentary resentment. You see, the thing of greatest importance in setting limits for children is the implied assertion: "I care. I care too much to allow you to do this to yourself. Therefore I shall determine the boundaries you're as yet unable to set." Again and again boys and girls come before the juvenile courts of this land who have not yet had anyone who cared enough to blow the whistle on their behavior.

Sometimes parents set limits out of other motives. Because parents are people they are easily hurt and frustrated. There are certainly times when those feelings color or even dominate their actions. That includes the various forms of punishment they inflict upon their children. In most cases we more or less successfully keep those emotions in check. In situations where that control is frequently lacking a child begins to feel that he as a person is only important in terms of his behavior. In the extreme, a child may discover that no one really knows he's around until he does something wrong. Logically, if pathetically, such a child may conclude that the only path to recognition is misbehavior. The tendency to deal with behavior rather than persons in a family situation may lead to quite different experiences. "I just can't understand it; we've given Peter everything," said his mother in an interview.

"Everything?"

"I mean his father and I have bought him things other boys never dream of owning. We fixed up our basement, got him a pool table and John even let him have an old broken-down car to tinker with to keep his mind occupied and out of trouble."

"You were worried about his getting into trouble?"

"Well, you see he never did mind very well, and . . ." Pete's parents had become increasingly concerned about his behavior. Their decision had been to try to manipulate that behavior by giving him trinkets to "take his mind off" unacceptable pursuits. Pete, incidentally, had learned a little reverse English and occasionally threatened to misbehave unless he got what he wanted. The result was a game of cat-and-mouse at which Pete's parents with increasing frequency were the losers. Actually, the boy's parents had never seen him as a person; they had never really accepted him. Then, when his behavior seemed to validate their unrecognized rejection, they were hurt and righteously puzzled. Upon an impassioned plea for advice, the mother was told there might be value in looking for special capabilities and accomplishments in Pete which she and her husband could encourage around home. There was no follow-up of the interviews. Two months later the boy was referred to juvenile court, and once again the mother couldn't understand the boy's actions.

Most parents have a big emotional investment in their children. Each has dreams for his boy or girl. He wants the child to avoid the difficulties he encountered as a child. He hopes his child will succeed in those endeavors where he himself failed. In short, he relives his life to a degree through his son or daughter. That natural tendency when it is out of balance, can also be dangerous. In the extreme it may appear as an unconditional demand for scholastic excellence, a place on the varsity squad or being "popular." This may have no reference to capabilities. When the child fails, the parent has failed. At that point where the parents' own needs become the dominant motivation for their supervision and control of their children trouble is likely to be brewing. That is where the young person becomes a pawn in the hands of a manipulative parent. Whether the child dutifully accepts this as the price of acceptance or openly rebels, he has thus been denied the essential experience of being accepted as the person he is. That, as we shall see later, is a tragic thing, from a theological as well as a sociological and psychological standpoint.

By the time the child is required to attend school he meets his third major socialization assignment. That is to make a meaningful adjustment to the world of the community. That world is full of strangers. Not many of them know him as a person, either. Yet in spite of this, he finds many of them acting toward him in ways which are to him vaguely familiar. He may not even realize this similarity consciously. However, observation of his behavior, makes it clear that many of his reactions to his teachers and other supervisors are those he has developed in his relationship with his parents. It is perfectly natural that this should be so, in terms of his limited experience to this point. Yet it is the more so in view of the parallels between the roles of mother and teacher, daddy and the policeman. Occasionally this must be called to the attention of inexperienced leaders of children. It's very likely that a good part of Mike's hostility toward school may be due to unresolved conflicts with his parents at home. Some of the trouble Miss Schwartz has with Julie may have little to do with Miss Schwartz personally. Very definitely, a significant part of required formal education is in the category of helping children wrestle with this third assignment. Learning in school must be largely in the context of a group. It follows, therefore, as it does throughout life, that relationships to others in such groups may have much to do with the quality and extent of learning accomplished there.

Things are quite different in the groups one meets away from home. There is an atmosphere of competition. Strangers are vying with each other for places in the groups and classes. This has to be without the direct involvement of either mother or daddy. More than ever, Anne's place among her peers and in her class ranking as well, depends upon her performance. She can earn a place for herself by virtue of the things she does. Her achievement spurs her toward further advances. As she finds herself able to merit the respect and approval of her classmates and her teacher she can reach out in confidence toward more difficult objectives. Each achievement can be a partial liberation of the child for further learning. Yet this depends to a marked degree upon some factors which are not always operative in a child's life. It presupposes that the child has developed such trust of mother that it is desirable to seek the approval and accept the encouragement of a mother figure like the teacher. It suggests that the boy or girl has already begun to accept certain disciplines as necessary steps toward achievement. It takes for granted, in fact, that a child has developed a satisfying idea of his own identity and his relationship to his brothers and sisters.

Our society won't wait. It demands of us that we keep step with its demands regardless of our progress in adjustment. Now if one further complicates the challenges of "normal" adjustments leading into adolescence by carrying along unsuccessful or even poorly begun social assignments, this should be cause for real concern. This is because the expected adjustments in adolescence have tremendous social implications for the young person. To face them without benefit of a satisfying understanding of one's own identity or a meaningful relationship with members of his family is like trying to build a house without tools. Bill gets to the point of using and misusing his peers in order to satisfy his own ends. In his home he's been similarly used as long as he can remember. Why shouldn't the same approach apply to his relationship to his girl on a date? Mary Jo has never had occasion to view herself as a lovable, valuable person at home. She is careless about her appearance and cannot be persuaded to explore and develop her real talents. She can't accept the fact that she can achieve and she shies away from activities depending upon acquired skills, both at school and among her girl friends. Bill and Mary Jo find themselves increasingly "on the outside, looking in" just when it means so much to relate meaningfully to their respective groups. A graphic picture of this state of affairs is available in the cumulative school records these two people make. At seventeen, as a sophomore,

Bill is dropping out of school . . . at the request of the school. Under-achievement, poor school citizenship, including the rejection of authority, and no extra-curricular activities figure prominently in his picture. Repeated truancy, the lack of any responsibility and inevitable scholastic failure actually indicate that Mary Jo had resigned from school long before her official dropping out on her sixteenth birthday. In these two instances each had the intellectual capacity but not the emotional equipment to relate or achieve. Thus they joined the growing ranks of the school "dropouts."

Some Further Warning Flags

There is increasing attention being given to the predictability of behavior in young people. To date, the hypotheses far outnumber the conclusions. Nevertheless, there is sufficient validity in the effort to warrant some brief attention to it here.

More specifically, there have been recently developed some intriguing efforts to predict the likelihood of delinquent behavior in young persons on the basis of knowledge about their early family relationships. If what we have been saying is true, then such tables may further emphasize and clarify the significance of early relational experiences. Most of these tools have grown out of analyses of the case histories of those found to be juvenile offenders, school dropouts or emotionally disturbed persons. Probably one of the best known devices of this sort was developed by the Doctors Glueck of Harvard University. This world-famous husband and wife team spent ten long years of careful study in the preparation of a device which when applied to six-year-old children can predict the likelihood of future delinquent behavior. The instrument is the fruit of thirty-five years of careful research in the fields of juvenile delinquency and adult crime and more recently, a herculean study of 1,000 boys. The latter turned up statistically significant differences between the delinquent and non-delinquent boys that paved the way for the Gluecks' "Social Prediction Table." The discovery that 50 percent of all delinquents start to get into trouble before the age of eight and that 90 percent before age 11 drew the Gluecks' scrutiny to factors operative in the lives of children under the age of eight. In the words of Mrs. Glueck, "The striking role of interpersonal family relations is the genesis of delinquency; the very evident lack of close relationship between the fathers of delinquents and the boys; and the revelations of an almost complete lack of family unity";[1] these led to the separation of five factors as complementary indicators of trouble to come, given a continuation of the extant situation at the time of examination. Very briefly, the relationships involved are these:

The father's discipline
The mother's supervision
The father's affection
The mother's affection
The family's cohesiveness

Time does not permit nor does present purpose warrant an explanation of the precise means by which these relationships are evaluated in the use of the table. Two sorts of tests of the usefulness of the prediction tool have been made. Once the $350,000 study of the 1,000 boys was completed, the researchers set about applying their conclusions retrospectively to children in Boston and New York about whom they had much case information. In 90 percent of the instances they could have predicted accurately the delinquency which in fact occurred in the course of touch with the children over a period of about ten years! Under the New York City Youth Board in 1953 a further evaluation of the table was begun, and is now soon to be unveiled. In 1960 the Youth Board reported that the instrument had already proved itself 87 percent accurate, with three years to go. Moreover, the boys were at that point at the age where the most serious delinquencies begin. Comparable studies in France and Japan are indicating that this Social Prediction Table has clear validity in other cultures as well. It looks as if we have in our hands the prototype of tools by which to glimpse future behavior, given a continuation of the present relational circumstances in a family's experience. This could revolutionize social welfare. Some criticize this as a determinist view of human experience. Possibly it may tend to modify some interpretations of the doctrine of Free Will. On the other hand, it would appear that it also points persuasively to the urgency of purposeful change of the quality of foreboding relationships in order

[1] Thomas B. Morgan, "Now We Can Spot Delinquents Early," *Think Magazine*, March, 1960, p. 2.

to avoid indicated trends of behavior. Something can be done about unhealthy relationships. Thus, if we have tools with which to warn ourselves of growing danger (devices accurate 80 to 90 percent of the time), then it behooves us to *use* that information! There is much more to be said on this, but that will be postponed for later chapters. In dollars and cents such information is expensive. In 35 years, the Glueck team has spent over a million dollars on research relating to penal and correctional treatment and the causes of delinquency and crime. Yet of far greater value is the possibility that with this sort of knowledge we may be much more able to prevent the occurrence of juvenile delinquency and adult crime; we may be able to help persons heading for trouble toward new wholeness in life.

This is by no means the whole story. Perhaps it is only an introductory though terribly significant chapter of it. We have been saying in this chapter that the already complex "normal" developments of late childhood and adolescence can be and often are upset by the absence or distortion of early and essential interpersonal relationships in the family. We have emphasized the crucial significance of a satisfying understanding of one's own identity, of positive adjustment and relationship to the tiny, intimate circle of the family and later, to its extension, the community. We've taken note of the fact that society imposes these assignments upon each individual in quick succession early in life. Though they demand a lifetime of effort, good progress on them is expected by the beginning of late childhood. We shall see more clearly as we proceed that among those who have little success with these assignments is the vast majority of the boys and girls who are found by our courts to be delinquent. All this ought to be convincing us that valid ministries with mixed-up young people are not as simple as they are sometimes said to be. They are in fact even more complex than the problems of the persons for whose benefit they are designed. That is because in the course of those ministries we involve ourselves. Now we shall concentrate our attention upon those mixed-up boys and girls whose reaction to their problems is in terms of delinquent behavior.

CHAPTER THREE

The DELINQUENT SOLUTION

Now that we have provided a generalized background for our thinking, let us move from common human experience to the more specific situation of the juvenile delinquent. We shall be concerned with the methods by which the delinquent attempts to solve the fundamental problems which beset him. There will be a greater amount of firsthand illustrative material used, and in general the framework for consideration will be much smaller. Our chief interest will center about the manner in which the delinquent person views and attempts to adjust to the expanding world about him, and to himself.

First a word concerning the title of this chapter. The phrase is borrowed from the fifth chapter of Albert Cohen's thought-provoking book *Delinquent Boys*.[1] The first sentences of that chapter are perfectly fitted for this point in our discussion:

> The delinquent subculture, we might safely say "the delinquent solution," is a way of dealing with the problems of adjustment we have described. . . . The delinquent subculture deals with these problems by providing criteria of status which these children *can* meet.

Baldly speaking, the delinquent solution is largely an *unsuccessful attempt* at solution of adjustment problems. This will become more evident toward the end of the chapter as we consider some of the inadequacies of the delinquent "solution." This distinction must be clear before we begin, else our vision may be somewhat distorted.

The "delinquent solution" is merely the manner of approaching adjustment problems which is the hallmark of delinquent society. It is that meaning which we shall intend to convey throughout the remainder of the book, in speaking of the "delinquent solution."

[1] Cohen *op. cit.,* p. 121.

Delinquency is Natural Behavior

We noted in the closing portions of the preceding chapter that pre-adolescence and adolescence incorporate the last of three major adjustment periods in life. The first involved the establishment of one's identity. Second was the discovery by the infant that he is not a solitary monarch ruling over the world as he knows it, but the child of a mother, and indeed a member of a family, upon which he is extremely dependent.

Later, in the period with which we are particularly concerned, this person, who is for a time neither child nor adult, is asked to extend the horizons of his total life experience to the community and to society as a whole. Although this is required of every mature person, it is by no means a small thing, nor is it easily or quickly done. Imagine then the predicament of the individual who has not yet been able to make adequate adjustment to the first of these stages of orientation.

This is precisely the situation of the delinquent or potential delinquent. He is still functioning as if the entire world revolved about him; as if it were indeed his world. People and things about him appear as means to immediate ends, particularly his own individual pleasure. He sees little reason why his desires ought not to be satisfied directly and as soon as they make themselves felt, without regard for the inconveniences or pain this may cause others. Too often this disregard for the welfare of others is considered as a symptom of inner evil and depravity in the delinquent person.

Actually this is the most natural behavior in the whole of human experience.[2] This is the a-social code with which the infant is equipped at birth; in fact this is the attitude of every new-born animal. One of the basic facts of human existence is that social behavior must be learned. It is natural to expect that some individuals will learn earlier and with greater facility than others. On the other hand, that person who fails, whatever the reason, to become socially orientated is not demon-possessed or even anti-social. He is still operating under the very natural code with which he first en-

[2] Clyde B. Vedder, *The Juvenile Offender* (Garden City: Doubleday & Company, Inc., 1954), "Delinquency is Normal Behavior" by Hertha Tarrasch (reprinted from *Focus*, Vol. 29, July, 1950, pp. 97–101), pp. 19–25.

tered upon the voyage of life. This is one of several facts about the "delinquent solution" which are not commonly known or appreciated.

All too often the proposed treatment of the delinquent demands the administration of stringent discipline in retribution for the specific delinquent acts committed. The idea of belated education and help is lost in the desire for revenge by the offended individuals and the community. This is not to deny that a part of the learning process involves the administration of firm discipline and basic controls. Any thinking mother can testify that discipline must play an important role in the infant's first attempts to assert his demands over hers and those of the family. Neither then, nor in the later adjustment period ought the central purpose in this action to be that of retribution, however. For the child whose only home training has been severe punishment for his offenses, full adjustment may be extremely difficult. This is true even if he submits momentarily to superior forces or authority.

The mother is the first authority figure to play a role of importance in the infant's life. This is to be expected inasmuch as she is the one who supplies all his needs during the first months of life. Normally he establishes with her a relationship of such strength that he is able to sacrifice or postpone the gratification of his own demands in order to assure himself of her love and approval. Now consider the plight of the child who early becomes aware that he is unwanted, that there is nothing he can do to elicit love and approval from his mother. The only attention he receives from her is vengeful punishment when he offends or displeases her. Rather than striving to control some of his instinctive desires for gratification he may very likely begin to pursue these goals more feverishly, knowing that by this artifice he can at least gain attention, though it is only expressed as punishment. At the same moment, the punishment which he receives may serve to allay a bit of the guilt he feels for offending and opposing her. Essentially then, the lack of a close relationship with the infant's mother may be an incentive to behavior which is better described as *anti*-social than a-social.

Small wonder it is then, that the child who has never evoked genuine love and approval from his mother, or from some other substitute in the family, may have great difficulty in adjusting to any other authority later. A few years ago I saw this vividly evident in the conduct of a delinquent boy fifteen years of age who was an illegitimate child. He came from a broken home where there had been the further complications resulting from the remarriage of his mother. The boy had been involved in very intense rivalry with the other children in the family. He had been described by the youth service board of his state as a "stubborn child and a runaway." Psychological tests showed that he had many positive capabilities. Yet this boy had nothing but resentment for society, as a whole, particularly anyone in authority. His expressions of this hostility were at times rather frightening to see. Again and again he asserted that the only way he'd be happy would be for everyone to leave him alone, and actually to allow him to do just as he pleased without interfering in his activities. However, since he had no feeling but deep hatred for all authority, this would have amounted to his trampling any and all who interfered in his pursuit of his still infantile efforts to satisfy his normal impulses. Though physically and mentally this individual was no longer a child, emotionally he was still an infant who had to learn to control his natural impulses. An evil person? Not at all. He was merely arrested in his emotional development to the extent that he was still "doin' what comes natur'ly" without realizing the need for controlling his behavior.

The Relationship of Reality and Authority in the Delinquent Solution

The matter of the delinquent's adjustment to the rights and authority of the community must be seen also in relation to his conception of reality. We have noted that one of the distinguishing characteristics of late childhood and early adolescence is that of a search for reality. However we further noted an exception to this rule in the area of social relationships. There, due to a lack of accuracy in the time concept of the child, his outlook is very *un*realistic. He is unable to think clearly except in terms of the moment at hand, when it comes to personal and social relationships.

. . . during later childhood the concept of time is not highly accurate. Children during these years remain primarily interested in current happenings. . . . For this reason it seems likely that they do not have the ability to understand social behavior that depends upon well developed concepts of time. The limited concept of time may thus be related to the "unsocial" behavior and "subversive" standards of these delinquent children.[3]

For the child who in adolescence has not begun to advance beyond this point in his development, those activities which do not hold out immediate benefits are worthless, and have little if any appeal. Yet that sort of "long view of things" is the basis of realistic, mature social living. Thus, a common quality of the delinquent solution is the tendency of its proponents to "want *what* they want *when* they want it," i.e., immediately. I saw this time and time again in my work in Boston's South End. In weekly experimental group therapy sessions such remarks as the following were made repeatedly: "Hey Doc, I don't see why I gotta keep comin' to these meetin's; they ain't doin' me no good!" or, "You said these meetin's was goin' to help us, but we just sit here and _____ around all the time. When you gonna *do* something?" and, "So the guy swipes yer shirt, an' you know he done it, so you mess him up good; what *else* is there to do? What would *you* do?" and, "The _____ food is _____! The only way we'll ever get a change is to have some action. Maybe if we begin to pull the _____ place down around their ears we'll get a change!"

However, in real life, persons in authority, representing the community are telling the older children and the adolescent that they must forego some of their desires temporarily in order to realize other "preferable" satisfactions later. No wonder that the child is led to ask, in one way or another, "Who is this who interferes with my pursuit of pleasure and tells me that it is better to look ahead for some of my much-needed satisfactions?" The child who has not yet made adequate adjustment in the first test period of life wonders about the validity of future promises, and still more, why he should have to accept the authority of society for his behavior. For him the present is all-important; for him, this alone is the essence of reality. On the contrary, this is a most *un*realistic outlook, from the standpoint of the mature person. The mere say-so of the community or of its repre-

[3] Vedder, *op. cit.*, "Probation: The Art of Introducing the Probationer to a Better Way of Life," by Elizabeth R. Glover (reprinted from "Federal Probation," Vol. xv, Sept. 1951, pp. 8–12), p. 391.

sentatives isn't sufficient to persuade the delinquent of the unreality of his approach to life. The rule of thumb for the delinquent culture is still the old pleasure-pain principle which governs very early childhood. Thus the troubled juvenile looks upon parents and the community alike as self-appointed agents of inhibition, or, in plainer language, "kill-joys."

Some Questions Toward Which the
Delinquent Solution is Directed

To speak of a "delinquent solution" implies that there are riddles, problems or questions toward which said solution is aimed, and this is certainly true with respect to the experience of the juvenile. We have already mentioned some of these problems in the first chapter and the remainder of this book will deal with various proposals aimed at their solution.

We are fundamentally concerned about the ministry of the Christian Church to the juvenile delinquent. First, we must have clearly in mind some of the major problems and needs of the young delinquent, and furthermore, the methods by which he has sought thus far to cope with his problems. Thus the time is right for us to acquaint ourselves with some of the tentative answers involved in the total delinquent solution of the juvenile's problems in adjustment. Only when we understand the central problems he faces as well as the means by which he has attempted to solve them can we hope to know where to begin our ministry in Christ's name.

"Who Am I?"   One of the first and most important questions to face the juvenile is, simply, "Who am I?" No doubt the reader has never heard youngsters on the street corner or in school phrasing the question in these terms. Neither has the writer. The truth of the matter is that most of the deepest questions of life are not asked point-blank, or in a few concise terms. Yet for purposes of discussion it is necessary to use a sort of verbal shorthand, in order to focus our thoughts within a manageable area of concern. So I say that a major riddle confronting the juvenile is that of his particular identity.

The picture the individual has of himself is of real importance in the character of his behavior. The self concept is held by many, especially the adherents to the school of client-centered therapy, to be a central factor in the total development of his personality. Carl Rogers, the father of this school, pictures the end point of personality development as being

> . . . a basic congruence between the phenomenal field of experience and the conceptual structure of the self—a situation which, if achieved, would represent freedom from internal strain and anxiety, and freedom from potential strain; which would represent the maximum in realistically-oriented adaptation.[4]

Certainly a great deal of difficulty can arise from a faulty concept of the self. Every person has some sort of definite picture of himself, which, though he may never describe it verbally, is quite clear to him. Each new experience one encounters is met by an I, and interpreted in a way that is dependent upon that person's view of himself. We act as the person we believe ourselves to be. What sort of self picture one paints is dependent upon such factors as one's level of aspiration, his sense of power or worth, or, at the other extreme, feelings of weakness, worthlessness, and general inferiority.

When the self-concept is distorted in any way, the individual may experience real problems. Thus, too high aspirations may have a depressing effect upon the individual who is actually incapable of reaching them. A conviction of unworthiness, on the other hand, may keep one from discovering and nourishing actual abilities and strengths. In my own associations with delinquent boys and girls in numerous and varied situations, I have been moved by the evident despair in the self concept most of these persons hold. They "know" they can expect nothing better in life than what they have already received. They now have a "record," and can expect that this will make them appear as lepers before most of society. They have been institutionalized as "problem children"; they don't feel that they can even measure up to the standards of their own peers. Some of their misconduct is actually a result of their trying to confirm the rejection of society and their own poor opinions of themselves. It has been very evident that any program of help for these persons must aid them first to more realistically evaluate themselves and their ability to improve upon these several predicaments.

[4] Carl Rogers, *Client-Centered Therapy* (Boston: Houghton Mifflin Co., 1951). See Chap. 11 "A Theory of Personality and Behavior," especially p. 532.

In the earlier portions of the book we noted that each juvenile finds himself in a veritable no-man's land between the camps of childhood and adult society. He is, as it were, a man without a country. He wants no more of childhood, and yet he is unable to merit acceptance into the adult world. He can no longer be judged as a child, but somehow it is believed that he ought to be measured by adult standards of thought and behavior. Though he is accorded some adult privileges, many others are denied him. He may have become of adult size, physically speaking, but he doesn't quite look the part as yet. He is told and too frequently reads in books about people his age, that he is passing through the "problem age" and that he will one day grow out of it.

For many adults the juvenile is a problem, but, more especially, the young person is a big question mark to himself. He must ask some other very frightening questions, in the light of the place he is accorded by those about him. Is he really an outcast? Are the changes which are coming over him depriving him of a place in life? What is there about him which has separated him from both children and adults? What's wrong? Will he ever become an adult, or has he somewhere got sidetracked in the course of his development? These questions might be posed by any juvenile. Now look again at the delinquent youngster or the pre-delinquent who has identified himself with the delinquent society, whether or not he has been apprehended for illegal behavior. To a further degree he has probably already experienced definite rejection by adults and adult-oriented children's groups. In a group session with several delinquents trying to see and deal with their mutual problems, one of the boys bitterly commented, "Hell, we aren't people—we're *teenagers!*"

The further inference in this remark was that in their experience, adults frequently used the words "teenagers" and "delinquents" interchangeably. His sense of lostness is complete. He may never have actually belonged anywhere or "been anybody" as far as anyone else was concerned. What could be the cause of such rejection of the child? Why has he been shunned all along the way? Is he perhaps some kind of misplaced creation dropped by chance into a place where it is at last clear that he does not belong? Possibly this all appears to be more in the nature of a caricature than a description of actual experience. If so, I recommend a careful reading of the excellent article in Clyde Vedder's book *The Juvenile Offender,* entitled "Delinquency from the Child's Viewpoint."[5]

For a year I had a detached assignment with a gang of delinquent boys in Somerville, Massachusetts. At first their questions seemed directed toward finding out about me: "Where'd you say you come from?" "Hey, how come you come over here with us every week? How much you gettin' paid?" "You goin' to college over there?" (Harvard University was close at hand—maybe I was just writing a thesis about them.) Later, it dawned on me that these boys were really asking questions referring primarily to themselves. Could it be possible that this guy *didn't* have an angle? Naw—there *had* to be some trick to it; nobody'd ever be that interested in them. They just couldn't believe anyone could find any genuine concern for *them* just as they were.

Some answer has to be found to this basic question of identity. It cannot be ignored. No one of us, child or adult, can stand for long in any place without knowing who he is. Yet any approach to delinquency which is founded purely on the administration of retributive discipline actually demands that the delinquent do just that. The juvenile with his poorly developed time concept, must answer this question without delay, and the "delinquent solution" offers quick "answer." It creates a name for him, and quickly transforms him from a nobody into "someone who *is* somebody." I am not speaking at this point merely of gang associations, although those experiences may be involved. I *am* referring to the more comprehensive sort of thing which Cohen describes as the delinquent subculture. He clearly shows that the two are not one and the same in the following quotation:

> Our delinquent subculture . . . is not a disembodied set of beliefs and practices, but is "carried" and supported by groups with distinctive organization and distinctive personnel. A position in this organization or affiliation with this or that particular member may offer other satisfactions which help to account for the participation of certain members but do not help to explain the content of the culture in which they participate.[6]

[5] Vedder, *op. cit.,* pp. 62–68. "Delinquency from the Child's Viewpoint" by Leontine R. Young (reprinted from *Focus* Vol. 30, May 1951, pp. 69–74).
[6] Cohen, *op. cit.,* p. 150.

It must be understood, when it is said that the delinquent solution holds out the offer of identity to the "lost" individual, that all this happens *only within the realm of the delinquent subculture.* That very identity in this area often brings complete rejection from other more acceptable circles. Nevertheless, from the standpoint of immediate, tangible solutions, the delinquent thus finds himself a place and a name, where he seemed to have neither before. He has subscribed to, or more accurately, he has committed himself to an entire way of life, represented by the over-all delinquent solution. Thus, wherever he goes he is one of that number. He knows that he is quite certain of a place, of being someone in the delinquent society within a given community. Even when he is for a time cut off from associations with others like himself, he can content himself with the knowledge that in the eyes of some of his delinquent friends he *is* someone by virtue of his unacceptable actions. Even those who have ignored or positively rejected the delinquent find now that he is someone with whom they must reckon. From a negative standpoint, there is an added distinction of having incurred the wrath of society by turning to delinquent behavior. Most children much earlier learn that when all else fails to attract Mother's attention, misbehavior will usually succeed, even if that attention only consists of disfavor and punishment. Certainly the delinquent solution does offer the nameless juvenile one sort of identity. We shall discuss a bit later the inadequacy of this and other suggested answers to the adjustment problems of the juvenile incorporated in the larger "delinquent solution."

"Where Do I Belong?" Very closely related to the problem of the identity, and perhaps its twin, is a question to which we have already alluded, i.e., "Where do I belong?" It naturally follows that the person who has satisfied himself regarding his identity must find where it is that he has a place, that he really belongs. To be sure, that need is partially met in the very adoption of the "delinquent solution." That is to say that the individual, in claiming his identity through subscription to the delinquent subculture, has set himself a place where he can belong. Yet this is all on a general plane. One soon finds that the delinquent solution is not the solitary behavior pattern of one young person. In the midst of a social environment based on radically different foundations (as for example the reality, rather than the pleasure-pain principle), the individual can hardly hope to pursue alone a course which interprets society alternatively as a means to immediate ends or a definite hindrance. Though it would often be tremendously satisfying for the delinquent or pre-delinquent to stand apart and defiantly misquote the famous words of Admiral Farragut "Damn society! Full steam ahead!!" this is almost impossible for the individual.

There must be that group to which he can belong and by which his faith in the delinquent solution may be inspired and nurtured. He must, at all costs have a specific *place* in his own particular environment. It is at this point that the "carrier" organization mentioned earlier enters the scene. The delinquent solution demands more than mere lip service to its major principles. There must be a definite means for giving them expression, namely membership in a witnessing group. This is due to an extrusive trend in the delinquent pattern, the tendency toward uninhibited, outward expression of tension.

Sheldon and Eleanor Glueck have uncovered rather conclusive evidence of a basic difference in the way delinquents and non-delinquents attempt to solve their emotional conflicts. Generally the delinquent tends to "act out," or give vent to his difficulty, and also to accept more easily a code which permits such irresponsible indulgence. On the other hand, the non-delinquent is more inclined to turn his conflicts in upon himself and to develop strong inhibitions of a neurotic sort therefrom. This is due to an apparently further developed Superego among members of non-delinquent groups. Thus "delinquents as a group are less neurotic than the law-abiding boys."[7] Interestingly enough, this internalization of conflicts, while it is the more painful for the individual, is by far preferable to "letting off steam" in an uncontrolled fashion. From a combined psychological and sociological perspective the former mechanism is more healthful than the delinquent's solution. In fact it is therapeutically sound and in some cases necessary to help the delinquent develop a neurosis in order thereby to be able to reach him with other therapy. That is to say, it is sometimes necessary to build up the delinquent's superego to the point where it can internalize and inhibit his emotional expressions of tensions. At this more mature level, therapy can be brought

[7] Sheldon and Eleanor Glueck, *op. cit.*, p. 158.

to bear on the problems involved. As long as the behavior and the emotional responses of the individual are strongly extrusive there is little that can be done, from a therapeutic, or treatment standpoint.

When an individual "chooses" his *group*, the one in which he can best express himself and thus find a place where he "really belongs," there may be some *conscious* selection involved. However, one should realize that the decision to subscribe to the "delinquent solution" is not a momentary conscious choice. It is inaccurate to say that the delinquent is one who has sat down and carefully weighed the delinquent solution against others and then concluded that the former is more to his advantage. The choice is made slowly and it might be better described as a non-conscious evolution of behavior, or way of life. Over a considerable period of time, perhaps his entire childhood, the individual who has failed in his attempts at necessary adjustment, may appear to "drift" into a delinquent type of behavior. Actually he doesn't just drift into this way of living, but, without being consciously aware of it, he grows into it, under the increasing pressure and direction of his unconscious desires, which are clamoring for expression.

Now, at the point where he decides he wishes to belong to a specific group he is faced with some *conscious problems*. Suppose that the group he is considering is a gang with a reputation for considerable delinquency, and perhaps one or more practices of which the individual doesn't actually approve. Yet this group seems most capable of supplying something he needs; that is, it represents a possible solution to a particularly significant problem in his adjustment, though he may not recognize that problem on a conscious level. He must now balance his attraction to the group against individual practices of which he doesn't approve. The carrier group can satisfy only the common core of needs of its members. It may very well be that it incorporates in its total activities some practices or attitudes which are incompatible with the particular standards of its individual members.

The price, then, of "satisfaction" of this common core of needs is a part in all of the activities of the gang, even if only on a level of neutral toleration. Thus Maria may decide to go with a crowd of girls with a reputation for greater sexual license than she herself endorses, because this group does offer promise of acceptance and some understanding. In the same way "Scratch" may become a member of the "Panthers," an admittedly delinquent gang, although he doesn't feel just "right" about the fact that several of its members are known to be "on the needle." Here is a group which can fight back effectively against authority figures in a way that he cannot do single-handedly. This is one means, therefore, for him to cope with those demands of society which he refuses to accept. He can afford to overlook the addiction of several members of the gang while he gains valuable nourishment for his resistance to the pressures of adult authority which beset him.

Many variations of this situation might occur. There might be but one group or gang and the question that of joining or refusing to do so. That choice might be complicated by the threat of violence as punishment for not joining. In any event the decision finally becomes a conscious one, though of course many of the influencing factors that governed that selection may be of unconscious origin. Thus, the individual comes closer to actually facing the important question with which he is really dealing: "Where do I belong, here, within the limits of my own community?"

The very fact that specific members' needs vary from the group norm, and that each person has his own particular hierarchy of values, causes a new member to look about him in search of those whose particular interests and values come closest to his own. It is very likely that he will find that in order to meet the approval standards of the group, his own may have to undergo some alteration or be partly silenced. Thus, for example, Alec, a new member of the "Dukes" who is maturing later than the rest of the gang, accepts the group model of the ace street-fighter. However he can't yet see the value of heterosexual relationships for himself, though the rest of the boys are interested in girls. If he is to keep his place in the gang he will be wise to keep this part of his own "ideal picture of himself" a secret. Position in the gang will in most cases be the crucial factor in the making of this sort of decision. The individual must have a place in some group, and the price he will pay for it may be quite high.

Who Will Understand and Love Me?   As we shall note in the next chapter, the intimate contacts of gang experience are an extremely important aspect of the individual's life in the gang. It stands to reason that the most natural of these contacts will develop among those members having the most nearly similar interests and models. For one thing the individual is much in need of a model which is or might be popularly regarded by others. Then too, it appears that persons having like heroes, hopes and hatreds are most friendly and understanding. At a deeper level, which he doesn't recognize at the time, he is looking for support of what in psychoanalytic parlance we term his ego ideal. He has developed for himself a picture of the sort of person he would like to be, and now he is really seeking others who have made similar pictures of themselves and lend support to his model structure.

This term "ego ideal" is often confused with "conscience" (or "superego"), or general, intellectually learned standards loosely called "ideals." The superego is the set of internalized standards and values which the child takes from his parents. This transferal of values presupposes a very close relationship with the parents in which the child comes to identify himself with them to the best of his ability.[8] Thus, it is to be expected that where parent-child relationships have been poor or non-existent, the super-ego will be quite weak if it has any power at all. On the other hand, the child, on the basis of identification with *other* persons over a period of time, might develop for himself a picture of the kind of person he would like to be. Of course this "ego ideal" may be quite unrealistic, or beyond hope of attainment. It may be rather perverted in the case of unfavorable associations. An unattainable "ego ideal" may itself be a considerable problem to the young person. The woods are full of intellectual ideals, and perhaps it is because of their commonness that they are of little real significance per se, and of no further value to this discussion. (For a helpful treatment of the distinction between intellectually learned "ideals," the "superego," and the "ego ideal," see Wattenberg's *The Adolescent Years*.)[9]

Among delinquents, a common core of opposition to authority may tend to make a group model of the individual who is most successful in defying, "foxing," or evading authority. Thus the hero of one group of delinquents I have known was a boy who three successive times "cracked" the safe in the home where the group was in residence. The boy never found a thing in any of his efforts, but his standing in the eyes of the others was after that a permanent thing.

[8] Friedlander, *op. cit.*, p. 41.
[9] Wattenberg, *op. cit.*, Chapter XVI, pp. 309 ff.

Beyond these things, there is an undeniable comradeship in the intimate associations of the gang which is very important to its members, whether they realize it or not. Very possibly this is due to the similarity of basic home experiences of the young persons concerned. There is some truth to the adage "Misery loves company!" In the vast majority of delinquent case histories there is evidence of a broken home life. In some cases it involves desertion, in others divorce, illegitimacy, general incompatibility and other factors. The gang may be for many boys the first opportunity they have had for an intimate contact with anyone. Thus, at first, the gang may seem to offer a rather satisfying solution to the problem, "Who will understand and love me?"

Up to this point we have been dealing with some of the major questions underlying the efforts of the juvenile to adjust to the expanded horizon of the new world about him, namely the community, and society as a whole. For the individual who has failed to make adequate adjustment to his own family world, this later challenge is vastly greater and more urgent. We have seen some of the ways the "delinquent solution" seeks to find a ready answer to these questions.

The Wrong Answers

I emphasized earlier that the answers proposed by this delinquent "solution" are not real answers. They actually fall far short of the mark. Let us see how it is that these proposals are inadequate, before considering two questions for which this "solution" fails to suggest any answer.

In essence, the delinquent solution suggests that the delinquent is really an outcast; that he *is* nobody. It invites this nobody to add his nothingness to that of others, until for a moment, like a vast conglomeration of soap bubbles, they appear actually to be something. It says that these empty bubbles can prolong their existence by adhering to one another, and thus continue to trick people into thinking they still amount to something. Once deprived of the thin film of moisture of which they are composed, they are nothing. To change the figure, this delinquent lacks a simple knowledge of arithmetic which would recognize that twice, thrice, or many times nothing is still nothing.

One sometimes distressing but constant fact of life is that we must learn to live with all sorts of persons. One gains his very identity through his relationships with other people. If he limits his relationships entirely to one group he is only considered one of them and no more. He is lost in the sameness of that one group. The delinquent solution to the question of the identity of the individual is as totally unrealistic as the purported habit of the ostrich in hiding its head in the sand at the approach of any danger. We just can't escape facing life that easily. The ostrich is all the more vulnerable if it insists on closing its eyes to the danger about it. Even so, the delinquent who withdraws from the matrix of social living, only postpones and makes increasingly difficult the adjustments he must effect if he is ever to participate in life as a mature person. The longer and more completely the juvenile attempts to identify himself with the delinquent way of life, the longer it will be before he can persuade the adult community of his readiness to enter its ranks as a mature person. Moreover, as myriads of former delinquents will bitterly testify, the community seems often to have the proverbial memory of an elephant where a record of past delinquency is involved. In many instances this is taken to deplorable extremes, but it is nevertheless an inescapable fact. "Who am I?", the unadjusted juvenile asks. The delinquent solution answers "Well, really nobody, but why not join hands with others like yourself, and share our nothingness for a time, while we boycott the world which you say has closed its doors to you."

The unconscious dialogue continues, and we hear the question, "Well, where do I belong?" The reply comes quicker than before: "Why, try the gang from 'D' Street. They'll surely have a place." Of course! The chance to avenge rejection by the adult community, to say in effect, "I never really wanted to have any part of your old broken-down adult dictatorship!" Yes, and thus the chance to flout the very principles on which mature society rests! Yet, what will *really* happen? The nameless, unattached creature, in asking for a place in the delinquent carrier organization sacrifices what position he might have had prior to that time. Moreover, he takes up a new-found position over against society as a sort of enemy sniper. Thus he has descended from an admittedly low status in adult society to the very negative depth of a threatening enemy. His new station, the "place he has found for himself," is frequently recognized by its antagonism toward the very society into which he hopes eventually to be admitted.

So it is that the "delinquent solution" is no solution at all, but rather an unsatisfactory effort to provide some immediate answers to the central questions facing the juvenile whose searching is complicated by adjustment problems which have become especially acute. It ought to be evident from the preceding paragraphs why this suggested solution is most fundamentally wrong. It is simply that THE DELINQUENT SOLUTION FAILS TO TRANSPORT THE INDIVIDUAL FROM THE REALM OF THE *PLEASURE-PAIN PRINCIPLE* TO THAT OF THE MATURE, *REALITY PRINCIPLE*. It entices the juvenile to continue to seek immediate gratification of his needs with a minimum of pain and the greatest possible pleasure. The delinquent solution therefore bars the juvenile from becoming an adult in his thinking. It refuses to look beyond the moment at hand. It ignores two further questions the mature person must ask: First, "In what direction am I headed?" and, secondly, "Where will that road eventually lead?" The delinquent solution is inescapably bound to the continuing present; too near-sighted to see anything but an oblong blur in a tomorrow. It prohibits the taking of the long view of life, so necessary in mature, social living. It keeps him from taking into account the demands of society and of his own under-developed conscience. Before concluding, however, that gang association per se is valueless and dangerous, your attention is invited to the latter portion of the following chapter, dealing with the "Appeal of the Gang."

In answer to the question "Where am I going?" the delinquent solution actually replies, "Just don't worry; stay where you are; if society won't accept you as a mature person, don't have anything to do with it." It invites the juvenile to be content to remain forever an immature person, and to shun responsibility in all things where his desires are concerned. In the last analysis then, the delinquent solution refuses to recognize the importance of the question of where the delinquent is going, or to concern itself with an answer. By the same token it fails to hear the closely related query, "Where will this finally take me?" Since "the future" is a threatening word, from the standpoint of the delinquent solution, the problem is considered non-existent. Therefore, it must be realized that this way of life is more nearly a way of death. It leads absolutely nowhere; rather it remains inert while all of life rushes on. The man who is late for his train realizes that the more of a start it has, the fewer are his chances of overtaking that last car on foot. Such is the actual plight of the person who continues in the delinquent pattern. It leads nowhere, and thus falls far behind the ongoing progress of adjusted, socially mature living.

We have discussed some of the major aspects of the delinquent "solution" to the intensified adjustment problems raised in the first chapter. These have included suggested but inadequate answers to the questions, "Who am I?," "Where do I belong?" and "Who will understand and love me?" We have noted that the chief flaw in the delinquent solution is that it fails to help the individual beyond the very immature stage of unadjustment which operates solely on the old Pleasure-Pain Principle. Two very significant questions it therefore overlooks are thus, "In what direction am I going?" and, "Where will this take me eventually?"

The inadequacy of this approach naturally leads one to inquire, "Well, *is* there a solution or a means to some sort of answer?" This will be the concern of the last two chapters, where we shall be dealing especially with the ministry of the Christian Church to the juvenile delinquent. Now let us look at an important part of most juvenile experience—the gang.

CHAPTER FOUR

The JUVENILE GANG

"Wherever Two or Three . . ."

"Get off! This is our Jungle Jim and only the ones we say can play on it. Becky and Alan and Greg and Linda and me can only play on it, but not you."

So says an uninhibited four-year-old, experimenting with the new identity he is discovering in his peer group.

One member of the nominating committee of a church youth fellowship observes: "We can have only one treasurer so we might as well choose. Maybe if we make Dick treasurer he'll start coming every week." Marcia replies, "I don't think many of us would flip if he did. Now if you do the same with Gary I can name six girls who won't miss a meeting!"

In the later stages of an experimental group therapy session with troubled teenage boys, one boy who is hesitant to reveal some uncomplimentary feelings before a recorder finally precedes his remarks with the words "Oh, if *you* gotta have this stuff, that's different. You're a bug doctor. That's your business. You probably have to have this stuff to help us, but we don't want *them* (the staff) to go listening to everything we say, so's they can laugh and take it out on us if we say somethin' they don't like."

Almost from birth each of us is involved to one degree or another in group experiences. As has been noted in the preceding two chapters one of the most significant features of preadolescent and adolescent experience is being part of a peer group. Almost without exception, teenage young persons attach themselves to one or more groups. At first these groups are sexually segregated. That, we have seen, is due to several factors, notably sex differences in the rate of physical maturing and the awkwardness and lack of savoir-faire which accompany the advent of secondary sexual changes. Gradually there develop heterosexual groupings toward which a majority of boys and girls gravitate. Nevertheless, most young people maintain relationship to both sorts of circles through life.

Among the several groups with which one has touch there is usually one he thinks of as "our crowd" or "our gang." This is the group with which one has the greatest affinity. Perhaps it's a street-corner play group. It may be a church youth group or a gang with a reputation for stealing and the use of narcotics. Of course, some junior deacon or his mother will be horrified to hear such groups mentioned in the same breath. Seldom does one refer to a church fellowship as a gang! The trouble is our habit in common parlance to speak of gangs only when referring to bands of juveniles known for their delinquent behavior or to adults involved in organized crime. Yet, a brief glance at some basic features common to all may remind us again that when we speak of juvenile or adult offenders or other hard-to-reach persons we are not talking about another kind of creature which exists in some equally strange medium apart from our own. Rather, we are thinking about persons who engage in many of the same relationships and struggle with some of the same basic questions as we.

Regardless of the locale, behavior, values or social status of a given gang or organized group, certain things about it are bound to be true. It follows then, that any really significant effort to deal meaningfully with individuals, or the groups to which they belong, must be based upon a working knowledge of the nature and functions of gang associations. More of a readable nature is written about gangs which engage in delinquent behavior than about other groups. Thus, it's natural that in this chapter we shall frequently use as a springboard insights drawn from observation of groups whose activities are usually delinquent or criminal. No person can be understood apart from his relationships to others. This is especially true of the young persons with whom this book is centrally concerned. Neither they nor any of us do many things all by ourselves.

Delinquencies, as well as non-delinquent acts, are commonly committed by youths operating in small groups; the "loner" is a relatively rare case.[1]

[1] Vedder, op. cit., p. 154.

We could dismiss the matter of gang relationships in a single paragraph if some of the most common assumptions about them were accurate and adequate. We could say that any gang is mob psychology in action. We could say that gangs are the progenitors of delinquent behavior and that the solution to the problem of delinquency is the abolition of all gangs. Yet we have embarrassed that easy conclusion by suggesting the possibility that in a real sense a church group could be thought of as a gang association! Furthermore, who would be so presumptuous as to try to do away with all gangs in the first place? For that matter, what are we really talking about when we speak of gangs? We need some sort of descriptive peg on which to hang our thoughts.

What Is a Gang?

Many still insist that a gang is an organization of criminals banded together in their antisocial activities by the knowledge that there is strength in numbers and the "right" contacts. They speak of blackboard jungles, of leather jackets, switchblades and sex parties. They point to notorious gangs and syndicates like those of Chicago at the turn of the century, and to later information about the "Mafia" and to current reports and investigations relating to the "Cosa Nostra." Impressions of this sort are gathered from hearsay, cheap fiction and a smattering of accurate information. It is a common opinion that gangs are not merely a-social groups, but antisocial, dangerous organizations. This "ain't necessarily so." In fact, gangs continually perform some extremely valuable functions for their members and afford many worthwhile and needed experiences in group living.[2] (Perhaps that will momentarily soothe the hurt feelings of offended churchmen who are still upset by the idea that a youth fellowship is a sort of gang.) More of this will be evident when we address ourselves to the appeal of the gang.

Let us begin, then, by examining one useful definition of a gang as put forth by Frederick Thrasher in his still-classic book on the topic. He states that the gang is an

. . . interstitial group, originally formed spontaneously, and then integrated through conflict. It is characterized by the following types of

[2] Vedder, *op. cit.*, "An Approach to Anti-Social Street Gangs" by James R. Dumpson (reprinted from *Federal Probation*, Vol. XIII, Dec. 1949), p. 162.

behavior: meeting face to face, milling, moving through space as a unit, conflict and planning. The result of this collective behavior is the development of traditions, unreflective internal structure, esprit de corps, solidarity, morale, group awareness, and attachment to a local territory.[3]

Perhaps one of the most striking features of this definition, from our present standpoint, is the absence of any reference to criminal or delinquent behavior. In point of fact, the preceding definition might well apply to many sorts of groups even to some youth fellowships and other church societies! Thrasher nowhere states that the gang is a criminal organization, nor does he even list delinquent activity as a characteristic of the collective behavior of the gang. Let it be clearly understood that the delinquent acts of a given gang are but one aspect of its total activity. A careful reading of the above definition would lead one to expect what is in fact true, that delinquent behavior need not have any part in the life of a specific gang. This cannot be over-emphasized. It should be more clear in a discussion of the genesis and development of the gang, and in the later section of this chapter dealing with the appeal of the gang.

Note that in the above definition Thrasher stresses the fact that the gang is generally an interstitial group; that is to say, it is born in the "in-between" sections of the community. This seems natural when one considers that persons in this predicament, in terms of either geography or social interaction, usually feel themselves to be "men without a country"—without a sure place. For a penetrating discussion of the great importance of the matter of status to the juvenile, the reader is invited to read Albert Cohen's book *Delinquent Boys, the Culture of the Gang*.[4] He stresses, for example, the major conflict which faces the individual who must make a choice between the contrasting value systems of two groups in which he seeks status. A compromise frequently costs the total loss of status in both. The decision to subscribe to the code of the one brings a denial of status or even clear rejection from the other. Thus it is that the juvenile has to choose sometimes between the approbation of adult authority and that of his peers, and a preference for one likely to be attended by disapproval and even punishment by the other.

[3] Frederick M. Thrasher, *The Gang* (Chicago: University of Chicago Press, 1927), p. 26.
[4] Cohen, *op. cit.*, pp. 129–135.

Repeatedly in some therapeutic group work with delinquent boys, that very dilemma was painfully evident to this writer. From the beginning, the group code of reaction centered about open hostility against the authority figures involved. Gradually, the boys began to change their individual responses toward partial acceptance. However, at the first point where these changes were consciously recognized by the group, the boys frequently went to extremes to show each other that they were still rigidly holding to the old code of hostility. Under these conditions both the therapist and I as process observer were threatened, called all manner of names, and in other ways reminded that the boys had elected to seek first the approval of the group, in spite of the possibility of disfavor or loss of status with us as adults. The immature individual cannot "sit on the fence" in this kind of situation.

One possible alternative for those who wish to avoid either extreme in such a situation is the formation of still another group with others of the same convictions. Cohen points to the formation of the Oxford Group and Father Divine's Kingdom as examples of this tactic. This reaction can sometimes be witnessed in a church or social group where a few individuals find themselves in an age level or other point which falls just between that of the major groupings of which the society is composed. Mutuality of interests, local experience, problems and ambitions naturally lead to the spontaneous formation of a small alliance or sub-group within the wider circle from which they somehow feel remote. This phenomenon lends support to the timeworn proverb "Birds of a feather flock together." Gradually the experiences of such an inner, more intimate group tend to give rise to the development of a hierarchy of interests, values, and preferred activities. Before a great deal of time passes, some factor in the sub-group value code, or consequent activity resulting therefrom, usually meets with opposition, and a conflict is experienced. This may involve changes or sublimations of code, if the sub-group decides to bow to the larger group and its standards, or varying degrees of opposition, even to secession from the parent group. The result, especially in the latter case, is a further integration of the small group, giving it strength and form. Thus the "Nifty Niners" might have developed from a nucleus of nine members of the "Green Hornets" who persistently stole, though the Hornets' code frowned upon thieving. Now the "Niners" hallmark is stealing, particularly shoplifting. This is a continuous process, and, if unimpeded or deprived of constructive channelization, may lead the way toward more serious behavior symptoms.

Children in neighborhood play groups together cultivate certain modes of behavior that are incompatible with adult values and standards. They must discover, however, that their right to freely swing their collective fist in any and all directions terminates at the tip of society's nose. Thus, perhaps a neighborhood play group is reprimanded for running through a corner hedge in the course of their games, or for misusing public or private property. At the outset, the a-social character of their behavior may be quite innocent. However, considerable resentment and hostility may be aroused by efforts to curb these activities. Children thus disturbed can't declare open war upon the police or a coalition of their parents, and yet somehow this "attack" by the latter demands an answer, a defense. One possible course of action would be for the group to continue to pursue the same activity, being careful to do so without being apprehended. This sort of reaction is full of adventure. It becomes a game in itself, to see how far or how long this behavior can proceed before someone is caught. This writer recalls such games in a high-school study hall, supervised by an inexperienced teacher, dedicated to the detection and punishment of rule violators.

When a member of the group is apprehended and punished, the entire membership may be further offended and threatened, resolving to avenge the misfortune of their comrade. Frequently it is in this manner that the play group begins to evolve into a more solidly-knit gang. Let it be noted that this type of development is *natural*. The observant parent, in a family including more than one child, will note such behavior at times within the four walls of his own home. For the child, and for all of us in our cliques, clubs and societies, yes, even our world family of nations, this is a long and painful kind of lesson to learn. We might wish that the child would clearly see his real problem from the first and immediately make a full positive adjustment to it. Yet one difficulty some people have in work with youth groups is the fact that they expect immediate results. No music teacher who introduces his new pupil to piano for the first time assigns him Chopin's *Polonaise in A Flat* for his second lesson.

The conflict between a play group or developing gang and the adult world frequently involves an individual's vested interests, public or other authority figures or a rival group in a nearby territory. Whatever the case, the experience draws the group together, strengthens and solidifies it and encourages a growing loyalty to it on the part of all its members. If this process is not given some constructive direction, if the opposing individuals or group continue only to attack the youngsters, the above development can reach serious proportions and result in delinquent behavior. Thus we have noted patterns in the development of the juvenile gang from beginnings in local play groups. Let us now glance at the basic organizational structure of the full-fledged gang.

The organization of the juvenile gang is strictly informal and very susceptible to change. It is a plastic, changing sort of relationship which helps to hold the group together. Nearly always there is one leader, or "head man." He is in command of the group by virtue of their common approval and consent to follow him. While leader, he makes the decisions of the gang and, unless his position is being challenged, his orders stand without question.

Usually the leader is accorded his position on the basis of demonstrated leadership ability, in athletics or some other preferred group activity, like prowess in fighting. The choice of the leader is made informally. In more carefully structured gangs the leader selects an inner circle of lieutenants to assist him in the administration of his power, and, on occasion to advise him in the making of decisions. Each of these lieutenants is usually charged with a specific task, though this depends somewhat upon the degree of development of the gang itself. Thus in a given gang there may be a "war general," a "light-up man" and contact men for maintaining relationships with other groups.

The next level of membership involves the rank and file group— the bona fide members in good standing in the gang. Among them are small groups which are gangs-within-gangs. These corner groups meet more frequently and often engage in more specific activities on their own. However, in time of need, as in a "rumble" or war, they automatically unite with the larger gang as a unit.

Finally there are the "fringers" and hangers-on. These are individuals and small clusters of persons who only take part in the life of the larger gang when a "big show" of some sort is on. This group often includes girls, who serve the dual purposes of sexual outlets for the boys, weapon carriers and lures or spies in inter-gang conflicts. It must be added that the degree of organization and individual responsibility to the group depends upon the stage of development of the gang. (See Thrasher's discussion of the major stages of gang development.)[5] Thrasher's definition of the gang listed several characteristics of gang behavior, and first among them was the experience of face-to-face meetings and associations. The relationship of the members of a gang is no mere chance acquaintance of persons in the somewhat distant, uninvolved manner common in many school associations. In part, the gang represents the means for an intimate level of sharing and understanding. Yet it may be that its full membership is seldom called together for meetings. Total gang membership may number from fifty to more than two hundred, but the most frequent and often the earliest associations of its members are usually among much smaller, more intimate groups of boys. Here frequent and prolonged associations during leisure time draw boys closely together. If the individual's experience at home, in church (if there is a connection there), at school, or in various social groups of the community, has been that of rejection or the lack of warm, satisfying acceptance and group participation, this continuing association with boys who *do* accept him, is going to fill a great need for intimate contact and sharing. Here in the smaller circle of regular neighborhood associates, the individual finds others who are facing similar experiences and discovering that which they have so needed but never experienced. Here a fellow can be "understood" and know that he is appreciated (though evidence of same may escape the casual or uninitiated observer).

We have already mentioned the role of conflict in gang life and the unifying influence it has upon the interests and the behavior of the members. In an informal corner gang with a minimum of structure, outside conflict may be about the only adhesive ingredient in the relationships between members. This writer recalls the tendency in one such group to direct hostile feelings toward fellow members when there was no common enemy to battle. Occasionally the worker had to intervene to protect one boy from the aggressive behavior of

[5] Thrasher, *op. cit.*, pp. 58–76.
See also Kitty Hanson, *Rebels in the Streets: The Story of New York's Girl Gangs* (Englewood Cliffs, N.J.: Prentice-Hall, Inc., 1964), pp. 6–8.

fellow gang members! Yet, in a fight, they were all one and as loyal as if they were all one family.

Of great importance in the life of the gang is the development of a specific gang tradition, or, as the gang members may say, a "rep." As a play group evolves into a gang, certain interests take precedence in the minds of its members. There are some activities which afford more fun and satisfaction than others. As this preferred behavior is repeated and perfected, it becomes more and more a distinguishing characteristic of that gang's life and contributes to its uniqueness. The reputation itself in turn frequently contributes to the status of the group as a whole, and, consequently to that of its members in the eyes of their peers. Moreover, in the idle hours spent "hanging around" exploits which have afforded greatest enjoyment or excitement become a source of mutual pride and an identifying badge for the members themselves. Thus, the activities of the gang, and particularly their conflicts with outside forces, magnified by the memory of these escapades, weld the group more strongly together, strengthen their spirit, morale and general group awareness. This is as true of socially well-oriented groups as of delinquent or other gangs.

Still another characteristic of gang life is almost universal. That is the matter of the close tie to a specific locale. When this writer was a group worker with the previously mentioned gang this became dramatically evident. First, it was obvious that the boys became greatly excited by trips which covered a distance of two or three miles. This was a long trip for them. Furthermore, in other parts of their own city they were quite lost. When they were asked by the leader for directions they were quite unable to oblige. Their entire world was a circle with a radius of no more than ten blocks and having as its center "their" corner! Gang associations seldom arise out of school associations, but rather the leisure time gatherings of young people in their own immediate neighborhood. (Schools usually draw children from a much wider circle.) Usually the gang defines its domain or "turf" in the community on a clear-cut geographical basis, and the boundaries of that territory are respected by other gangs and outsiders alike. Any violation of these established bounds, whether through mere trespassing by members of other gangs, "invasion" of the territory by a hostile gang, or dating "across the border," frequently leads to full-fledged "rumbles" or gang wars.[6]

[6] Hanson, *op. cit.*, pp. 72–78.

From these observations of gang experience and behavior we may conclude that the most important thing about a gang is that it is a *way of life*. Any given juvenile gang is unique, and has a tradition of its own, growing out of specific mutual interests and exploits. It is a spontaneously generated association of young persons in a clearly defined, local area to which they are attached. It usually involves intimate and intensely loyal relationships which are most evident in conflicts with outside forces.

The Appeal of the Gang

Why do children join gangs? If group associations and activities are usually in some way involved in the delinquent acts committed by juveniles, why in the world do youngsters join gangs? What does one find in the gang which apparently cannot elsewhere be obtained?

The answer must be hidden among the relationships into which one enters in the gang community. A bit of the solution is inherent in the last two words of the preceding sentence. Every person has certain basic needs in his life. The interpretation of these needs and efforts to satisfy them may vary as the individual matures. Common among us all, though, is the desire for genuine affection—to love and be loved by another person and groups of persons; to be accepted for what one is, to be considered of worth in the eyes of others. In short, one needs to experience membership in a community of persons. The gang is one such community.

Some parents and other adults appear to be unable or unwilling to introduce children to this very necessary ingredient of a wholesome life experience. In such a situation, it is often the children who must, therefore, seek group relationships on their own. It is partly for this very reason that the adolescent is extremely concerned about his relationships to his peers. He must have some place among the people who talk his language and share his type of problems and thinking. Concern with taxes, politics, and other adult matters is all part of a world to which he does not yet belong and in which he is not presently interested. The things which hold his interest are competitive games, various forms of excitement and thrills, conforming social relationships and the varied uses of leisure time which "older" folks often seem no longer able to enjoy.

Let the reader be assured that there are few things more hideously painful than the experience of the child who feels totally alone—apart from the world of both adults and other children. Jack is the name which will do for a boy who survived that awful loneliness and later dedicated himself to protecting others from it. He was a member of a high-school-age youth group in a church situated in a rather well-to-do suburban community. He was the youngest of three children, and the only one who had not planned on attending college. (His older brother had been awarded a full scholarship to M.I.T.). His youth group put an extremely high premium on intellectual acumen. Its outstanding leaders were the older sister and brother of the boy in question. He himself had left school to procure a job where his non-verbal abilities could be realized. He spent some time in a correctional home as punishment for an offense committed with the only company in which he was able to find some degree of acceptance, a gang whose "rep" was for stealing cars. This made him a social black sheep.

In contrast to others in the church group, Jack's chief asset was his remarkable manual dexterity. However, this was of little value to the group as a whole. The boy was physically well-built and attractive. Obviously, he could easily have bettered his brother in any physical combat or competition, yet he often accepted a public tongue-lashing by his older brother. The brother had behind him the irrefutable authority of their parents. Thus, by all the prescribed standards, Jack was a misfit. He simply didn't belong. During a party at which I saw this development in process, the boy remained continually on the fringe of activities. Not the slightest indication was once available that the two group leaders were members of his own family. He was totally ignored. This boy desperately needed someone, some group to which to tie, but instead he experienced the exact antithesis of this situation in his associations with the church youth group and even his own family. Such a young person will continue to look for such an association until he finds it, no matter how far or how long he searches. Perhaps some who read this have never experienced this sense of aloneness, but particularly for the adolescent it can be a hellish torment. Worse than physical starvation, this gnawing hunger often horribly disfigures and distorts the mind and spirit of the afflicted person. The gang holds out a partial remedy for this very serious ailment, in the form of intimate face-to-face relationships and the sharing of common experiences. For the individual who is playing the "left-out" position in the game of social living, the gang has a definite and strong appeal, and performs for him a service of immeasurable value.

Then too, the gang represents considerable power and prestige to its members. In the first place, a boy such as the one described above, needs to have some status among the majority of his peers in the juvenile community. If this is impossible for acceptable reasons, membership in an unacceptable sub-group may afford an inviting alternative. He then becomes someone to be reckoned with, as a member of a power-wielding gang. To be sure, his status in the wider community may suffer if his gang is not acceptable to the community, but very likely the loss of status in the wider group is a cheap price to pay for a definite place in a smaller group or gang. He has proved himself able to meet the group's demands and they have agreed that he can be entrusted with the gang secrets, and participate in its privileged activities. Therefore, the individual gains strength from the power of the gang as it is represented in the estimation of the wider juvenile community, and a real acceptance *within* the circle of the gang itself.

We have already spoken of the basic social assignments given each person in life. Continued frustration of a child's efforts to discover his own identity, plus the absence or distortion of fulfilling relationships can hinder the development of effective controls for his feelings and behavior. Nevertheless, from a practical standpoint, he knows that certain behavior just isn't tolerated. Thus he learns to check some actions merely because in so doing he avoids painful punishment or retaliation. He becomes "wise" to outside limits; he learns the necessary rules of the road he takes. He observes them simply to assure his own comfort and safety. For example, he can fight openly with another child, but not so with his parents or against society as a whole. In point of fact, there are many threatening persons against whom the child is at a loss to know how to fight or resist. Society makes them immune from frontal attacks. Somehow, somewhere the child has to vent his stored-up feelings. Yet for a single child this often appears impossible. He lacks the necessary confidence and the backing of like-minded comrades, to effectively express his rebellion. Furthermore, he has no standards by which to justify such expressions of feeling. He needs the power of a group behind him,—the power of community which endorses *this* kind of behavior in spite of the dictates of the larger society.

> . . . we believe . . . that for most delinquents delinquency would not be available as a response, were it not socially legitimized and given a kind of respectability, albeit a restricted community of fellow adventurers.[7]

Let it suffice to note here that the gang makes a strong appeal to the individual from the standpoint of the various sorts of power it represents. Incidentally, a closely related aspect of this whole matter is the protection a gang assures its members. One basic understanding between members of a gang is its commonly-accepted mutual defense pact. Thus, at any time of threat, an individual member can count on the loyal support of the rest of the gang, and frequently, even when the individual is known by the gang to be deserving of some sort of punishment. (Of course, if he has violated the gang's own behavior code, that is another matter.)

I recall vividly an interview with a teenage girl on the accident ward of a large city hospital. She had been rather badly cut up in a knife fight. Following a long and heated exchange of questions, accusations and contrived answers between the girl and a police officer there was a later opportunity for another conversation, while her wounds were being dressed. I did little but listen.

> He thinks he's so smart. He don't know nothin'! I didn' tell him nothin'. They're all the time comin' round an' tellin' us off. He thinks he can scare me into tellin' what happen. I ain't tellin' *no* one . . . not you, either . . . but I'll tell you one thing. . . . You see what happen to me tonight? . . . Well, about *tomorrow* night you doctors gonna be *busy!* Some of *them* will be in here tomorrow night and you'll have a lot more sewin' to do. We don't need no _____ cops to fight our battles!

This girl's gang relationship lent her strength to rebel rather openly against an officer and to boast about the assured vengeance to be wreaked upon her assailant by her gang. Thus the gang members enjoy a certain degree of safety, afforded in the understanding by all

[7] Cohen, *op. cit.*, p. 135.

"outsiders" that an attack upon the individual will invite retaliation by the gang. In all, the gang is a power unit, and a source of great security to its members.

We cannot overlook still another appealing factor in gang life. That is the element of continual fun-seeking, which is usually the original pursuit of the playgroup out of which a gang springs. That search is not dropped when the playgroup develops into a gang and the individual enters adolescence. It doesn't require exceptional powers of observation on the part of the child to realize that the opportunities for fun, adventure and excitement are many times multiplied when one is a part of a group which pursues similar goals. The possibilities are endless. Stories of the escapades of romantic figures and groups both in fact and fiction are often an inspiration for play activity of a gang, whether that activity is delinquent or not. The possibilities run from King Arthur's Knights to Ali Baba and the Forty Thieves and back again. Particularly appealing are the exploits of such famed figures as Robin Hood or Jesse James. Gang names, like "The Alley Rats of the Round Table," "The Forty Thieves," and "The Robin Hoods," give an indication of the thirst of juveniles for adventure together in their various activities.

Not long ago I was talking with a detached worker in one of our eastern cities. He informed me that one of the discouraging facts which hinders effective boys' work in an area where morally responsible behavior is the exception, rather than the rule, there is little one can offer to a boy which is more appealing than the enticing benefits to be accrued from "playing the game" with the "big boys." A plush job, protection against conviction in the case of arrest, favors and privileges—all these are strong incentives for a boy who may already model much of his behavior on that of the successful "smart guy," the racketeer, or the fellow in the "driver's seat" of the local political machine. Here is a chance for escape from the dull monotony, continuing poverty and general despair which often plague socially and economically deprived children. Here is the chance to "live it up" . . . to put one's dreams into action. Here is a scale model of the real thing. The obligations incurred for such benefits are of little concern to an adventure-seeking boy, and frequently the errands and "jobs" gang members may be encouraged by the racketeer to carry out, may be appealing and adventuresome in themselves.

We began this chapter by examining the basic nature and development of the juvenile gang, and we have considered something of the appeal of the gang for the individual who is a prospective member. Now we shall briefly focus our attention upon the predicament of the hard-to-reach "fringe" person as he confronts society as a whole and the Church in particular. Then we should be ready to consider the theological basis for the challenging ministries to which this book is dedicated.

CHAPTER FIVE

The LONELY ROAD To JERICHO

A man was going down from Jerusalem to Jericho, and he fell among robbers, who stripped him and beat him, and departed, leaving him half-dead. Now by chance a priest was going down that road; and . . . he passed by . . . likewise a Levite . . . saw him . . . and passed by.—Luke 10:30–32

The road to Jericho, like that between most communities in Jesus' day, was evidently a lonely one. To travel it alone, even in broad daylight was risky. There was the constant possibility of being ambushed by bandits. Furthermore, if one became ill or was injured it might be a long time before anyone would come along who could render assistance. Then, when one did come he might not stop. Then as now, passing strangers were not likely to risk very close association. It just wasn't done in proper circles. Furthermore, it was an old trick to feign injury with intent to waylay a well-intentioned but careless traveler!

Perhaps the reader at this point thinks to himself, "Yes, and probably among such marauders would be many like those about whom this book is particularly concerned!" That is probably true in part. Certainly it represents the sort of thinking which for so long has governed the reactions of society and the church in particular. Almost never, when we are interpreting this story, does it cross our minds that the plight of the *wounded man* on the road to Jericho is not unlike that of the hard-to-reach young person in our society today! We tend to think first of *protecting* ourselves from such "problem" people and, if we are offended, how to punish the one who has hurt us.

The tendency to deal with offenders out of fear and vengeance has been in vogue for a long time. Justice has thus largely amounted to a search by society for self-protection and immunization against attack.

At times of greatest insecurity, the unbridled fear of the criminal has led society's protectors to abandon even the pre-Christian arithmetical code which demanded "an eye for an eye and a tooth for a tooth." The criminal has long been thought to be an evil, vicious creature who could only be dealt with in terms of punishment appropriate to his crime. In days gone by, one of the most common modes of punishment demanded by the community was the death of the offender. This treatment suddenly and finally ended the threat of said person posed to the community. Until comparatively recent times even children were treated in this fashion when convicted of "criminal" behavior. In thirteenth century England, only children under the age of ten and one-half years were considered to be immune from criminal prosecution on grounds of non-responsibility. From then on, "minors were liable to be punished, capitally, as otherwise."[1] About this time there developed a Council and then a Court of Chancery, which was designed to protect those classes and persons who were incapable of defending themselves against undue treatment under the common law courts. The Council and later the court received the petitions of such groups and persons and its jurisdiction tended to be much more "elastic" than that of the common courts. It particularly dealt with situations involving infants and their estates under the authority of *parens patriae*, the power of guardianship over persons under disabilities. This principle is a foundation stone of the modern juvenile court. Actually this often amounted to extra protection for the property rights of the well-to-do infant. Later the concern extended to the person of the child.[2]

In spite of the above precedent, further enlightenment has been slow to occur. Benjamin Fine cites evidence of rather recent treatment of children as adult criminals:

> Harsh punishment of young offenders has been tried in this country and in many other countries, now as in the past and it just has not worked. Back in the early days of this country we found that children were treated as adult criminals. We have a record of a child of eight who was hanged for maliciously burning down a barn. A child of ten

---

[1] Tappan, *op. cit.*, pp. 167–168. (Reprinted excerpt from: Blackstone's *Commentaries on the Law of England*, 12th edition, with notes and additions by Edward Christian, Bk. IV, Chapter II, pp. 21–24.)

[2] *Ibid.*, p. 169.

was hanged for killing his companion. A girl of thirteen was burned to death because she had killed her mistress. In 1828 in the state of New Jersey a boy of thirteen was hanged for an offense he committed when he was twelve.[3]

Miriam Van Waters, in speaking of the relentless pursuit of the law after its basic logic ("Where there is crime or injury, there must be responsibility"), relates an unidentified case in which a sow was solemnly convicted and executed for having, with her litter of pigs, damaged a crop. Interestingly enough the litter of young pigs was spared because they were thought not to be to blame—not responsible![4]

In the first half of the present century, however, great strides have been made in terms of reappraisals of the raison d'être and the powers of the courts. In Illinois, in 1899, a state law was enacted which for the first time established a juvenile court for the hearing of the cases involving juvenile delinquents. This act followed by thirty years the first formal probation statute ever to be enacted in this country. The latter provided for a visiting agent to call on children in state institutions or in the charge of designated persons at least once in every three months in order to protect the total interests of the individual and the state.[5] Standards of theory and of actual treatment have been much improved since. Laws providing for the establishment of juvenile courts are in effect in all of the states today, and thanks to that example, juvenile court laws have been enacted in most European countries. However, as late as 1954 there were still twenty-one states which still permit some offenses . . . to be excluded from juvenile court jurisdiction or to be shared concurrently with other courts.[6]

Yet, in spite of the formal enactment of laws to establish a new code of treatment for the juvenile offender (there have also been noticeable advances in the recommended treatment of the adult offender), actual experience has lagged far behind. Thus, for example, the function of the juvenile court and the aim of probation

---

[3] Fine, op. cit., p. 141.

[4] Miriam Van Waters, Youth in Conflict (New York: New Republic, 1932), p. 147.

[5] Tappan, op. cit., "Appendix B," pp. 554–555.

[6] Vedder, op. cit., "The Juvenile Court in Retrospect" by Charles L. Chute (reprinted from Federal Probation, Vol. XIII, Sept. 1949, pp. 3–8), p. 236.

are usually misinterpreted.[7] The formal emphasis has turned from retribution to rehabilitation. The laws on the books are opening the way toward helping the offender to recover from the maladjustment which led him into trouble, and to return him to a responsible place in society. However, the general population is not yet convinced that this is actually the best procedure by which to deal with juvenile offenders. It is still difficult for people to understand in a specific situation that a given offender ought not to be punished for his crime, although in a theoretical discussion, the same people may affirm the principle of rehabilitation over that of mere retribution.

> The newer methods of treatment, probation, for instance, have come into existence not as a new form of punishment, but as means of re-education. The way in which these methods are applied shows that they are still widely considered as milder forms of punishment rather than as methods of re-education which can only be employed if they fit the individual offender and not merely the offense.[8]

General opinion seems still unable to free itself from allegiance to what many nostalgically describe as the "old-fashioned, woodshed school of discipline." The idea is that if the punishment for a misdeed is severe enough, the offender will refrain from ever repeating the act. Yet this does not happen. It is known that in England at the time when the penalty for pickpocketing was public hanging, the very ceremony of the hanging often proved a field day for other pickpockets among the crowd of onlookers![9]

There is something in this attitude which is worthy of careful thought. It has to do with the whole question of social responsibility. For too long this term has been generally interpreted as the fine art of not stepping on society's toes. When that standard is violated, society makes the individual "pay" for the disturbance or inconvenience.

At first glance the woodshed reaction seems chiefly to be that of mere retaliation. However, there are those who are beginning to suggest that there are deeper things involved, which, when better understood, help to account for the slowness of society to adopt new ways of thinking. As we have noted ourselves earlier in this paper, delinquent behavior is an expression of natural impulses which the

[7] Tappan, *op. cit.*, pp. 315–318. See also Fine, *op. cit.*, pp. 284–293.
[8] Friedlander, *op. cit.*, p. 3.
[9] Fine, *op. cit.*, p. 142.

individual has failed to learn to control. Consciously we say we are afraid for the future welfare of the community, if such behavior is allowed, and so we punish the offender. Yet unconsciously, there is a deeper level of reaction. If antisocial actions are not punished the individual super-ego suffers a considerable setback, and thus presently controlled impulses can threaten to burst forth and lead one into behavior which will invite retaliation by others against us.[10]

In an article entitled "Scapegoats of Society" Ruth S. Eissler adds a further dimension to our view of the offender against society. She suggests, with the supporting evidence of clinical data from individual cases, that delinquent behavior on the part of the individual may perhaps satisfy definite needs of others with whom he is related. She indicates that delinquency by one person may bring vicarious gratification to another person closely related to the offender. Thus the related individual can satisfy himself that he is innocent and only the offender is a criminal. Dr. Eissler writes:

> Thus for society in general there remains only one justifiable outlet for aggression which can be rationalized on the basis of morality and which can provide the desired relief by externalizing inner conflicts without creating conscious guilt feelings. This is the persecution of the wicked, the criminals, that group of individuals who commit violence, who break the laws and who do not conform to the demands of society.[11]

All this tends to make of society and the well-behaved person unassailable, almost holy creatures. The importance of the individual is lost in the mad rush to defend a challenged society. We too often conclude that the fact that a given individual acts in anti-social fashion is cause for condemnation. We punish the individual because he offends or defies society, because he has done what we have kept ourselves from doing. Psychoanalysis emphasizes instead that this behavior is but the symptom of the psychological illness of the individual, and it is to the illness that the psychoanalyst invites atten-

[10] Friedlander, *op. cit.*, pp. 191–192.
[11] Ruth S. Eissler, "Scapegoats of Society," *Searchlights on Delinquency*, ed. K. R. Eissler (New York: International Universities Press, Inc., 1949), p. 295. (See Henry Weihofen's *Urge to Punish* for a much more thorough treatment of this subject.)
Henry Weihofen, *The Urge to Punish* (New York: Farrar, Straus & Cudahy, 1956).

tion. We have made it a "sin" to affront society, and the zeal with which we have punished that sin has precluded any significant concern with the real needs of the offender. The following are pertinent snatches from a revealing paper on this very topic of Social Responsibility:

> . . . one cannot stress too much that the mere fact of the criminal's being anti-social is not considered to be a psycho-pathological phenomenon, and that even if it were, society is charged with the duty to rehabilitate the delinquent. . . . As a psycho-biological phenomenon he is a sick person. . . . As agents of society, we who would be the loyal protectors of society become unable to identify ourselves with those culprits, and therefore we are bound to fail both as healers and as sociologists, because one cannot heal . . . anyone unless one can identify one's self with the sick person in question, with the culprit in question, with the guilty one in question. The psycho-analyst's perspective can be broad and deep, and his performance creative and extensive only if his identification is with the person to be served and not with the disindividualized aggregate called society or history.[12]

This warning to psychoanalysts ought to apply to all of society, and certainly to the Church.

If the above is true, and the evidence is persuasive to this writer, the aforementioned disparity between theory and practice in the treatment of legal offenders may be expected to continue for a long time. No doubt the process of the re-education of the individuals who together make up society is really the first requirement, if we are to come to the point where we can actually begin to re-educate and rehabilitate the individual offender. That process is not easy inasmuch as the above-mentioned "scapegoating" is done unconsciously.

It is a means of considerable unconscious relief when someone is punished for behavior which another has only with considerable pain learned to control, but which the latter truly wishes he might still perform. The observer simultaneously experiences vicarious gratification of his inhibited desires, and yet is free of conscious guilt himself. Moreover, the conviction of the offender and his subsequent punishment strengthens the position of one's superego. Of course, without such punitive measures, one may be forced to return to the arena of

[12] Gregory Zilboorg, "Social Responsibility," *Searchlights on Delinquency,* ed. by K. R. Eissler, *op. cit.,* pp. 336–337.

his own self and become the actual combatant in the struggle where he was previously only a vicarious gladiator. This will not be easy or pleasant.

Even as this retributive reaction has been characteristic of much legal practice and of the attitude of society as a whole, it has been painfully true of the Christian Church. Inasmuch as the Church draws its constituency from the ranks of society, this seems a natural development. Yet the Church claims, through the grace of God in Christ, to be a community of transformed and transforming persons. Members publicly own the role of the good Samaritan, allegedly intent upon loving God and their neighbor. Nevertheless, history has witnessed many scenes which have been totally incongruous with that professed love of neighbor. Following the very severe persecutions which plagued and indeed threatened the very existence of the infant Church, the tables were turned. The subsequent denunciation of pagans, the vicious punishment of heretics, climaxed by the barbarous Inquisition of the thirteenth and late fifteenth centuries, were hardly convincing evidence of a boundless Christian love of neighbor.

The Church courts wielded great power, and at some periods amounted to the sole legal authority in the secular community. This was even true of the early settlements in the new world. Though the emphasis of the Church was ostensibly upon the administration of God's law by His chosen agent, there seems to have been more at stake. There was a fervent desire to protect the health and safety of the select community which was based upon these laws. How many "witches" have been tried and sentenced by the same basic sort of fear and insecurity which we have discussed!

All too often today the dope addict, the unwed mother, the juvenile delinquent and other of society's black sheep become the scapegoats, not only of the community at large, but the inner Church community. Many will cry that this is an unfair representation of the Church, or at least of certain specific church congregations. If this is so, and this writer desires convincing evidence of same, may their blessed tribe increase!

· Many an aroused layman will assert "There has never been a time when anyone has been turned away from the doors of Corner Church." At least two things must, however, be taken into account when such a statement is made. In the first place the person whose presence is not desired at any place seldom needs to be formally notified of that fact. It is painful and immediately evident, in most cases, in the personal relationships that the individual experiences. Thus the unwed mother would no more think of going to Corner Church than walking upside down. "I . . . I just couldn't face them, . . . there's just no place there for me any more," she'll explain to her mother. And, as far as real understanding and a genuine welcome are concerned, the unwed mothers and other untouchables are too often right about the lack of a place for them in the Church. How viciously and sadistically we treat the person who has perhaps been just a little less able to control the expression of desires natural to us all! We smile to see one child scolded for misbehavior by a chorus of children which is largely composed of those who were also guilty but not apprehended. Yet how often this is a realistic representation of what actually happens in the refined adult community!

Think, for example, what an excellent scapegoat the "juvenile delinquent" makes! He is forever guilty of spectacular, immature offenses. Certainly, this is where the scapegoat theory should break down. It must. After all, no adult would ever want to behave in such childish ways! At least, no adult could afford to be *discovered* at such behavior! Vicarious participation in another's delinquencies is one means of satisfying the urges to immature behavior which tempt the adult. Thus it is really a natural thing for the adult to keep himself, and therefore his family in a sphere apart from this threat to his emotional economy. This is frequently the actual practice in many of our churches. This tightly knit group can serve to mutually strengthen the controls of the members over the clamoring desires which continually demand expression. That exclusion, by whatever subtle means, serves also as a very harsh punishment of the offender who has been left out.

Furthermore, the satisfaction which probably accompanies a statement that "no one has ever been turned away from Corner Church" is a bit unrealistic. It implies an anemic attitude which is all too prevalent in churches today. It limits the church's approach to a passive reception of any who see fit to seek us out. This is one of the major difficulties, one of the fundamental failures in the particular mission of the church to the hard-to-reach juvenile and his group. The cold hard fact is that the delinquent just won't come to the

Church like flies to sugar. From their standpoint the Church has nothing to offer. This feeling is based on the lack of any previous significant church approach to their situation. There has been a frankly unrealistic flavor in most church programs according to the tastes of delinquent, generally lower-class persons. In a modern parallel to the scene pictured on the road to Jericho, we have made it known that we would provide the torn and bleeding delinquent a good book to read while he waits for the ambulance—if he lasts that long! We have tried to be available so that, if he looked us up, the delinquent could locate us, but *seldom have we sought to meet* HIM *where* HE *is,* where HE lives. When he has not been irresistibly drawn to the Church we frequently are tempted to conclude that the fault lies with him and his lack of response. "After all," we say, "if they won't take the help we offer, there is little we can do." If the tiny group of persons who became the nucleus of the new-born Christian Church had waited for the world to beat a path to their door, they would have been likewise disappointed. Rather, they were so convinced of the worth of what they had to share, that they went out and looked for ways to make the Good News available to those who would not, *could* not come. The Church, by and large, if it is to minister to delinquent society, must find a means of reaching out beyond itself—of making the Gospel of Life available to lonely rejected people. Our chief failings in the efforts we have made in the past have been the result of inappropriate language.

The Language Problem

Before one can function very effectively in a foreign place, no matter what his capacity, he must establish some means of communication with the persons among whom he will be living. This is just as true of the Church's approach to the hard-to-reach person for, we must face it—this is foreign territory for the Church as a whole. The reader may jump to the conclusion that I am referring to the inadequacy of strictly theological jargon in dealing with juveniles. Exclusive dependence on that sort of vocabulary has no doubt proved a handicap in dealing with youngsters on many occasions. One who knows nothing of the current specific lingo of the juvenile may be bewildered oftentimes by the things he hears. He may be somewhat further bewildered if he is subjected to some colorful cursing. Are we now recommending that in order to reach the hard-to-reach we must affect their vocabularies? Not at all. In fact, persons who attempt to do so often forfeit the respect of those they try to reach by this tactic. No, our language problems are more than a matter of the words we choose. The opening remarks of a Church school teacher to his class will illustrate the point:

> Class, our lesson today is about love, and . . . Johnny! If you don't stop that . . . all right! That does it! You get out of this class and don't come back until you're ready to behave yourself. Now where was I . . . Oh yes . . . we were talking about love, and our memory verse is . . .

The teacher was speaking two languages simultaneously, just as we all do frequently. Perhaps you thought you only spoke one language or perhaps even two; but two at a time? On the one hand our teacher made the verbal announcement of the subject, love. Yet as he did so he spoke in another language a message which was equally clear to the class and, in this instance the exact antithesis of his opening remark! The members of that class were far more likely thereafter to think of love as the reward for good behavior, something unavailable to a troublemaker!

The above incident is a key to one of the major languages most church people speak. In the context of congregational study or any other group experience, this functions like an unwritten contract. In fact this is so of nearly every group to which you belong. When you join it is clearly understood in almost every instance that certain kinds of behavior are henceforth expected of you. In order to remain a part of the group in question you do certain things. You will pay your dues or pledge and attend meetings faithfully. You will also refrain from doing (or being *caught* doing) certain other things. In some groups the penalty for failing to abide by these rules is formal exclusion from the society. In others, a sophisticated cold-shoulder accomplishes the same purpose. Very simply the contract, if written, would say: "Do what we do and you're in, but step out of line and you've had it!" This is to deal with persons only in terms of what they do. That is the way we usually treat animals. Why should it not apply to persons? Purely and simply because they *are* persons and need to be seen as the persons they are, rather than what their actions make people think they are! Not infrequently our actions are misleading and therefore misunderstood. A tired commuter found a seat on the aisle opposite a man and two whimpering children. It had been one of "those days" at the office. The father across the aisle seemed unable to quiet the children and their crying wore on the nerves of our commuter friend. Finally he leaned over and blurted, "Mister, can't you do something to stop your kids from whinin' and snivelin'? Some of us would like a little peace and quiet!" The man turned for a moment from the children and answered, "I'm sorry, but I don't know what I can do about it. You see, my wife was buried this morning. I . . . I don't think I'll be able to quiet them for a while."

Nora Stirling has written a playlet for the Family Service Association of America which nicely emphasizes several of the things we have been saying in this chapter. It is entitled *Boys at Large*. In it she particularly stresses that behavior is only symptomatic. It is a warning flag, telling of danger at hand. At one point the officer insists that although three boys were all involved in the same offense (symptom), each had a different illness. (The officer had good reason to know, too.) This is sound. When you go to a doctor with a temperature, he does not treat the temperature, but the sickness which causes it. The fact that someone is a "bad actor" is by no means adequate information upon which to base our dealings with him.

There are other languages which most of us speak which are in varying degrees foreign to those people whom we find it difficult to reach. One is conglomeration of middleclass values upon which we base so much of our thinking and action—things like creativity, initiative, adventurous individualism, stick-to-it power and the possibility of someday becoming President ("where there's a will there's a way"). Then there are those idealized virtues like close family ties, brother love and community spirit. These things have become so much a part of us that we frequently find ourselves lecturing spontaneously on them to children. Nevertheless, we often are astounded to find that these sterling virtues are unappreciated and even unknown to a growing number of children, especially those whose homes are in our growing inner-city ghettos. Studies coming out of the current Great Cities Project have made it evident that the teaching of inner-city children must involve recognition of the fact that many such children are economically and culturally disadvantaged. This has led to the development of revised curricula for public schools and religious schools. This writer has witnessed the discovery of such special need by suburban teachers of Weekday Released Time classes in the downtown churches of a city of only 140,000 people. One of them observed in bewilderment, "I've never worked with children like these. I've taught just as I always have, but some things I've always taken for granted just don't register with these boys and girls!" At this point the reader will find extremely helpful the resource papers gathered in the study book prepared for the 1963 Workshop on Children and Youth Not Served by Churches & Agencies in Detroit, sponsored by the Committee on Church and Agency relationships, in cooperation with the Department of Social Welfare, the Department of the Urban Church and the Central Department of Evangelism of the National Council of Churches, in league with the Detroit Council of Churches. Two brief quotations indicate the caliber of these studies and also illustrate the point just made:

> The gang, says Albert K. Cohen, now special advisor to the President on Juvenile Delinquency, is a group approach to the solution of the conflict between the status goals and problems of lower economic classes in a culture which increasingly is dominated by middle class values.[13]
>
> Most urban families are restlessly on the move, playing havoc with the assumptions on which the programs of educational institutions, churches, community life and even the family are built.[14]

When any teacher approaches pupils primarily on the basis of a clearly defined set of cultural values, those pupils who do not know those values are at a distinct disadvantage. Let it be emphasized at this point that such limitations are not the exclusive burden of inner-city people. In an earlier chapter we spent some time in discussing

[13] Resource Book for Workshop on Children and Youth Not Served by Churches and Agencies. (Workshop sponsored by the Committee on Church and Agency Relationships with the cooperation of the Dept. of Social Welfare, the Dept. of the Urban Church, and the Central Dept. of Evangelism of the National Council of Churches; and the Detroit Council of Churches.) 1963, p. 44.

[14] Ibid., p. 52.

the role of meaningful family relationships in the development of personal value systems. When such relationships are absent or severely distorted, one's value system is rather likely to deviate proportionately from generally acceptable norms. Thus it is that a language predicated upon values which are unknown or unappreciated by those we seek to serve may be at first an obstacle to learning and communication, if not an instrument of alienation. Illustrative of this is the reported plaintive question asked of a teacher who had been describing God as Father: "Does *he* come home drunk every night?" The questioner wanted no part of God as Father, for the word was the grim reminder of much unhappiness and pain in his own experience! We shall note later the use sometimes made of value conflicts in the testing of well-intentioned workers by hard-to-reach children.

Still another dialect tends to hamper the outreach of churchmen and others in youth-serving groups. It is the organizational approach, and has to do with two related things. First of all, in most churches and agencies we have a natural tendency to think in terms of concrete programs and well regulated procedures. This is natural, and, for the majority of persons this is a very satisfactory approach. Secondly, this sort of effort is easily tabulated; a measurable thing. Reports on these endeavors provide clear indices of achievement. This affords gratifying proof of conscientious stewardship. Such benefits are often indiscernible, however, when the programs involved are not so clearly structured. Recently, in two separate instances involving training for the informal use of volunteers in dealing with hard-to-reach children and families, the question has been raised, "Yes, but what are we supposed to *do?*" The idea of *being* a person who cares was too vague, too difficult to score. The thing to remember is this: as long as we carefully order and regulate every one of our institutional efforts there will be some we fail to reach, and among them will be a significantly high percentage of the persons with whom this book is particularly concerned.

The very programs we tend to prefer, those from which we can derive the clearest sense of achievement are the same ones which threaten and discourage the involvement of "fringe" children. There are several factors which contribute to this state of affairs. One is the fact that numerous rules and limits bespeak the presence of authority, and, in most instances, persons who wield it. For those who have difficulty in dealing with authority figures, especially those who affect the delinquent solution to their problems, any but the most minimal structure is a drawback in a program.

This does not mean, however, that such structure cannot be developed along the way. It only points out that programs geared for such children may have to begin on a rather fluid basis. This was borne out in a recent pilot effort to reach largely unreached older teenage boys in Evansville, Indiana. The vehicle for the effort was a very loosely structured athletic club program involving body building, through weight-lifting and fundamentals of wrestling. The program began with a mere invitation to make what the boys wanted out of the meeting time and the room they had been given. At first the leaders became disappointed and angry over the fact that the group was so unstructured. The boys arrived as much as thirty minutes late many weeks. They skipped sessions and were quite undependable. Frankly, the adults were tempted to "crack down" and set up some rules. Fortunately this did not happen. Instead, as they began to feel at home in the group and a part of each other, the boys themselves began to bring up the need for rules for themselves. Later, the adults had to suggest that they not make the rules too rigid! It took this group the better part of a year to get to the point where most children are when they join a club or church group program.

There is something else about clear structure and regulations. They demand a considerable amount of individual skills. This is as true of group and interpersonal relationships as it is of athletics. It is a mystery to inexperienced workers with delinquent or other hard-to-reach young people that these children often either avoid or mess up clearly regulated activities. Either procedure nicely hides the lack of necessary skills. This writer has watched numerous groups of delinquent boys on a basketball floor fail miserably at the simple requirement of making solo layup shots in an organized play period. Yet when there was free time moments later, they turned to a game in which they were sure enough of themselves to let go. It consisted of tucking the same ball under one's arm and charging the rest of the group to see how far one could go through the pile without losing the ball. This they understood and thoroughly enjoyed. What does this say? Merely that all of us need to be fairly sure of ourselves before we enter upon a new activity requiring special skills. Each of us hesitates on such a threshold. However, the person who really doubts his ability to do anything very well waits much longer and perhaps never participates. This further illustrates the significance of the self concept about which we talked at the end of the third chapter. If experiences in your life, at home and later in the community have led you to actually believe that your abilities and your worth as a person are about nil, it's unlikely that you'll be quick to accept invitations to join in activities that involve skills of any sort.

Therefore, to the extent that our programs are closely structured and carefully regulated we may lose the opportunity to serve the hard-to-reach person. Such structure is for many such people a procedural language as unintelligible as Greek.

To be a stranger in a land is bewildering. To be unable to fathom any of the languages spoken there is enough to produce feelings of deep loneliness. To be viewed with varying degrees of fear and of judgment because of one's actions, including those which grew out of these feelings, may lead to such a sense of rejection as to call forth defensive aggression or some sort of escape. We just don't think of the hard-to-reach person, particularly the delinquent, in the way that we do the wounded man beside the Jericho road. Yet actually, in several respects their predicaments are quite similar. A few lines come to mind here from the introduction to Fritz Redl's and David Wineman's arresting book, *Children Who Hate:*

> There is a great difference between a child whose basic personality is still in good enough shape to be approached . . . through the design of a benevolent institutional program, and the child in whom some of the normal behavior controls have already been destroyed by those who hated him so much when he was dependent and weak and who by now is but a *helpless bundle of aggressive drives.* (This author's italics.)[15]

A helpless bundle of aggressive drives! To be sure, Redl and Wineman are speaking of deeply disturbed children, those whose hate-filled behavior makes them the children nobody wants. Nevertheless the picture of need and helplessness applies more often than we realize to the children to whose salvation this book is dedicated. For

[15] Fritz Redl and David Wineman, *Children Who Hate* (Glencoe, Illinois: The Free Press of Glencoe, Inc., 1951), p. 22.

them, the modern road to Jericho is as deserted as the one our Lord once described. For a long time the few who have passed that way have been too much concerned with their individual safety and that of society to entertain thoughts of helping these wounded travelers. A few have hesitated long enough to prescribe some sort of medicine. Once in a while someone has stopped to apply his pet remedy. Those who speak have in most cases used languages which had no meaning for a stranger, so there is no way to convey the real needs to those well-intentioned wayfarers. When you come right down to it, we haven't said much about *why* anyone should bother to stop and try to help this stranger by the side of the road. Before going further, we owe ourselves an answer to that question. Thereafter, if there's a real call for such extraordinary behavior, we can talk about how we might proceed!

CHAPTER SIX

WHY STOP To HELP?

All right! So somebody's in bad shape over there in the ditch. That's tough. I'm sorry. But you've just been saying a good number of us don't even talk his language. I couldn't help him if I wanted to. I'm late now for the group I work with. I'll be a lot more good to them than somebody I don't even understand. And while we're on the subject, let me ask you something: Are you really sure we have any *business* getting mixed up with him? There isn't much you can *do* with somebody like him. We'd have trouble with him right off. I've seen the kind. He isn't interested in the same sort of things our group is. He wouldn't fit. Why kick up a fuss just because somebody we don't even know had some tough luck on the road?

Perhaps this imaginary conversation raises a few righteous hackles. Yet, the question is a good one. It is seldom voiced, but yet it frequently dampens the enthusiasm of potential helpers when it goes unanswered. The assumption which is inherent here is that there is something constitutionally different about the hard-to-reach person, and that therefore we may not need to assume responsibility for him. Certainly a reasonable answer to this question is essential to any worthwhile action we might take. Furthermore, that answer ought to be theologically sound. Otherwise, there arises the equally fair question of whether the *Church* has any real business getting involved.

We do too many things as churchmen today without any awareness or concern for the theological answer to the question "Why?" Perhaps if we asked it more often we'd be better able to establish priorities for the use of our time and talents. So many of us spend so much time and effort on the treadmill of activities which might best be described as nice-but-innocuous. To do a thing merely because we had the time and somebody asked us is not entirely commendable, if we have had opportunities to make other choices which would have put our talents to much better use.

Let's be more specific. Can children like these about whom we're concerned respond to a religious approach? Are their needs really the same as those of other children? They hardly seem even capable of religious experience most of the time. Listen in, if you will, to an actual conversation which took place in a modified group therapy session at the Charles Hayden Goodwill Inn for (teenage) Boys in Boston, Massachusetts.

Therapist: I guess you don't think much of having to go to some church on Sundays.

First boy: Well I s'pose you gotta have faith . . . (said in falsetto, to the amusement of the group).

Second boy: Oh who the _____ you kiddin', man! That stuff's for fags! (word for effeminate, homosexual or otherwise distasteful persons).

Therapist: Well, I see you don't buy this. What kind of things *do* you go for?

Second boy: Man, that's easy! Beer, broads (girls) and plenty of that nice green stuff that makes the world go 'round!

Third boy: (spontaneously and with feeling) _____! There ain't nuthin' in that jazz neither. You kill a fifth and it's over, 'cept the hangover; (many laughs) you have a broad and then you wouldn't spit on the best part of her; (no more laughs) and you latch on to a wad and kick it all in on _____, an' what you got left?

The conversation went on to other topics. The language used in the above exchange might at first keep one from the realization that these boys had for a moment been intensely involved in a deep theological discussion! This group was talking about the very same things which ought to be the concern of every teenage (or adult) church group in the course of its experience!

"Well!" you say, "*We* certainly don't make it a habit to discuss alcoholism, fornication and irresponsible spending of money in our groups!" Let's overlook the question of whether or not that is something to brag about. These boys weren't really talking about those things either! They were merely using familiar vehicles for their thoughts! We talked in the last chapter about some of the confusing languages we tend to speak when dealing with hard-to-reach persons.

That should cause us to look a little further for an effective language in which to begin some genuine communication. This chapter will suggest that such a language is available in a Christian understanding of the nature of a person, his relation to his fellows and to God, and the nature of the Church.

The boys in the preceding encounter were talking such a language. They were speaking eloquently, if indelicately about the basic meaning of life, their place in it and their relationships to each other. What more basic theological questions could they have raised in the space of two minutes? Their experience had been pitiable. They had been searching to find some meaning in life, some reason for being. They'd been trying to find out who they really were and what they were to those about them. Every time they had reached out for the truth about themselves it had seemed to burst, like a bubble, in their faces. All they had to show for their efforts were haunting handsful of emptiness. Even their extremely limited experience with church life had been frustrating. They had been looking mainly in the wrong places, true, but their search was nonetheless genuine. They deserved to know the Truth which, when effectively mediated, might have made them free. They, too, were created by God for that freedom.

They needed, as each of us does, to know their true worth as persons. This had never been revealed in their brief lives, so, many of them had spent considerable effort to convince the world that they really were important after all. Since they didn't actually believe it themselves, they were deeply suspicious of anyone who claimed an interest in them for what they were. They had never been worth much to anyone, themselves included. They'd *heard* that God loved them, but nothing had ever happened to convince them this was true. Certainly no one had ever substantiated this by his dealings with them. Here were young swans whose experience had kept them convinced they were some rather ugly ducklings. They hadn't learned the facts of life. They didn't know that they were God's children, created in His image, that they were brothers one of another. They desperately needed to receive the News about life. They craved that very wholeness which is the root meaning of the church word "salvation."

Repeatedly today we read in magazines and newspapers, or hear and see on radio and television frightening descriptions of delinquent and troubled young people. Such pictures may cause us to wonder how such boys and girls could be so inhuman, so lacking in normal feelings. In most instances much of the full story is omitted. For example, close touch with such boys and girls for very long makes it clear that these frightening children are often themselves frightened persons. They are afraid that the brittle shell they have built about themselves may crash in on their awful emptiness. This is in fact the basic spiritual predicament of any person who has not known for himself that he is of importance, that he is related to God and to his fellow men and that there is therefore purpose and meaning and hope in life. Such persons are on the outside, looking in on life, afraid of everyone and everything about them, afraid of themselves. They trust no one. Why should they? Experience has taught them it's extremely dangerous to trust anyone. Better to stay apart and avoid getting hurt . . . again. This fear can be observed in individuals and groups.

A few years ago after several hideous sex crimes, the sick person who had committed them scrawled a desperate message in lipstick on the mirror in the bathroom of the most recent victim. It went about like this: "Somebody stop me before I go any farther!" Who of us, for that matter, has not witnessed the mounting anxiety of a group which is beginning to get out of control and the subsequent easing of that tension when the leader, for their good, applies the brakes.

Following one of the aforementioned group therapy sessions at the Hayden Goodwill Inn, the group process observer happened to be the last adult in the lobby as the supper hour arrived. The staff and rest of the leaders had already gone on to the dining hall upstairs. The observer was talking with some of the boys when he realized that the two directly in front of him were now holding open knives pointed at his belt. The pair began a discussion about whether they would cut up and down or crosswise. There was a sudden hush among the thirty or more boys in the room, and immediately tension began to build. What had begun as a playful gesture now had become a major test before a group which would countenance no retreating. The boys were afraid of the consequences of persisting but more afraid of backing down. The observer, naturally uneasy, but also aware of the plight of the two and of the whole group, which could so easily be stampeded into a disastrous melee, needed some means for getting everyone off the hook. It happened that one of the knives in question was the sort having a serrated edge designed for the removal of scales from fish. Fortunately, this was a thing of genuine interest to the observer, and, after looking at it in the boy's hand for a time he asked to look more closely at it. Two or three moments later following a comment of appreciation he returned it to the boy, still open. This opened the way for a conversation about various sorts of knives and their relative merits. The appreciative use of what was otherwise a threatening instrument provided a positive means to quell both the boys' fear and the group pressure. This is only one sort of evidence that even the most disturbed outsiders wrestle with the same basic emotions as we. Endless illustrations could be drawn from real life to further prove the point.

Those fringe persons who stand outside and look in on church and other group activities do not do so because they have no *need* of the basic things offered there, or because they're fundamentally different. Rather, it is only because they cannot *accept* them on the terms we usually offer. We can preach at them till we're blue in the face, but unless we're able to act out the Good News, over a period of time, we'll never make even a beginning.

We'll include in the next chapter a discussion of the process of testing which develops when we approach such fringe persons and begin declaring our concern for them. Suffice it now to re-emphasize that these hard-to-reach children are *very* human and *very* much in need of what the Church has been commissioned by Christ to share.

Another major factor enters the picture when we talk about the theological and ecclesiological bases for ministries with hard-to-reach persons. It is the redemptive nature of the body of persons in Christ which is the Church.

In recent years there have developed many intense efforts to redis-cover the nature of the Church. This has been one of the fruits of the renewed ecumenical movement. One of the things that is being increasingly said is that the Church is mission. We have nearly escaped the limiting assumption that mission is what the Church *does*. Rather we are coming to understand that as we really become the Church we re-enact what has been done in our lives by the Living Christ. Reuel Howe, in his sensitive book, *Man's Need and God's Action*, puts it this way:

[God] speaks and acts through us, and we become the fellowship of the redeemed and the redeeming, the fellowship of the reconciled and the reconciling.[1]

That is to say that when the real thing happens, when the Holy Spirit in all its mystery and power returns us from our estrangement to our place with God, there cannot but be a comparably radical change in our actions. It can't happen without our becoming part of that same continuing work of the Spirit in the lives of others. When that occurs we are really becoming the Church. To put it another way, we can't be the Church without becoming instruments of God's reconciling action in the world. The reason we must enact the Good News with hard-to-reach persons, indeed with all people, is simply that we cannot fail to do so and at the same time be the Church! Yet too often, declares Reuel Howe, we say

"the world is not interested in what we have," and so we go into our churches and close the doors behind us. The clergy settle down to be chaplains to the faithful, and the faithful just settle down. Outside those closed doors go thousands and millions of men and women who in one way or another cry, "Please take me back." They do not know that they cry, or for what, or that the answer lies behind those closed doors. It is just possible that if we can hear their cry, they may hear our answer. Ours? No, not our answer, God's—God's answer to them through us, His Church.[2]

How ready we have been to dismiss the hard-to-reach as the "world" which is "not interested in what we have," and thus lost opportunities really to be the Church in the world! There is no man nor child who is not interested in discovering who he is and whose he is.

This chapter could have been a much more lengthy and scholarly treatise. It has not been intended as an exhaustive treatment of the subject. It is hoped that its brevity will not lead the reader to conclude that it is relatively unimportant, for its purpose has been the cornerstone of the entire book. A comment by the Rev. Mr. Henry Nichols, president of the Greater Philadelphia Council of Churches seems especially appropriate at this point:

. . . . we are here on business for the King; and if not, we have no business here.

[1] Reuel L. Howe, *Man's Need and God's Action*. (Greenwich, Conn.: The Seabury Press, Inc., 1953), p. 141.
[2] *Ibid.*, pp. 133–134.

God in His mysterious love has chosen to make persons His chief business—all persons. Our mutual predicament is our estrangement from Him. In Christ He has reconciled every one of us to Him. There are no exceptions. This is our one glorious story and our song. As that becomes real in our lives we cannot help but share the Good News. Only thus can we hope to be His Church—His continuing work on earth. There are those whose social estrangement makes especially urgent their need of the re-enactment of the Gospel. We have been calling them the hard-to-reach. We've been saying that the theological basis for our ministries with them is that of our entire mission for Christ.

Provided, then, that we accept the validity, and, in view of our frequent shortcomings, the urgency of incisive ministries with hard-to-reach children, we are still left with the question "How?" To that we'll devote the next chapter.

CHAPTER SEVEN

BINDING Up The WOUNDS

But a Samaritan . . . when he saw him . . . had compassion, and went to him and bound up his wounds, pouring on oil and wine. . . . Luke 10:33–34

Now we come to the point of discussing the actual avenues for mission that include the hard-to-reach young person. We have refreshed our memory about the developmental changes in process in the juvenile individual and some crucial factors which may influence those changes and his relationships as a whole to those about him. We devoted one chapter to the delinquent solution to problems of adjustment toward which many hard-to-reach children gravitate. We noted the universal importance of the gang in juvenile experience. We've had a look at some of the problems facing us and the fringe person as consequences of his decision to stand apart, and our own language limitations. Hopefully, we are now convinced that any ministries we might undertake with these persons derive from the inclusive character of the Great Commission, and the basic reconciling work of the Church as continuation of the Christ event in us.

The intent here is to be more specific. Frequently, books on related themes begin at this stage to list proposals for action that are so broad and airy that the reader finds himself yawning with increasing frequency as he reads, if indeed he does continue further. On the other hand, we ought to be careful not to assume that this means that we shall have touched all the concrete problems involved in effectively ministering to the needs of persons who are on the fringe of things. We shall merely single out some which are likely to stand out in these special ministries, and attempt to treat them quite specifically.

In the next place, since this book is part of a series on pastoral counseling, this portion will be geared especially to the work of a minister of a ministering church. It should have much to say to both the church and public school teacher, the youth fellowship advisor, choir director, teacher of weekday released time, club leaders, and every genuinely concerned Christian neighbor, but . . . first of all it has in mind the work of the Christian pastor.

Starting Just Where You Are

Perhaps what has gone before occasions surprise over the above sub-title. Our special concern has been hard-to-reach young people, and now it is suggested that a pastor begin his efforts where he is—in a church! We ought to keep in mind that the mere fact that one is a participant or even a member of a church group is no guarantee that he has been reached meaningfully.

In most circles, churches included, there is an individual or two who perennially play the "left out" position in group activities. Call them "wallflowers," "squares," "odd balls," or just simply persons who don't fit. They're there without a doubt. And great things can happen to them and to the group *right there!* Furthermore, you as a pastor can help it come about. This is no idle dream! Too many people throw up their hands in horror at the thought of helping persons with special needs in the context of ordinary group experience. Yet it can be done. It *has* been done, over and over again.

For years the Boston Children's Service, Inc. has maintained a "neighborhood group" program which works on this basis. When a child is referred to them he may be assigned a group worker, who in his neighborhood draws about him a peer group. None of the other group members are aware of the strategy. They choose an activity or interest and pursue it as a group under the supervision of the as-signed leader. The leader has been trained to be sensitive to the needs of the individual and the potential of the group to meet them effec-tively in the normal course of their chosen activities. This is a thera-peutic tool that works, and it can be employed in the existing organi-zational grouping of your church. After all, what do we mean when we speak of the church as a redemptive fellowship? Dare we count ourselves out as possible instruments of that very redemption?

An actual experience illustrates the point. Betty, a nineteen-year-old girl, returned home after consecutive commitments to the state

Girls' School and the state mental hospital. She was of medium height, but had a very powerful and heavy body. She feared no physical challenge. She had never learned to whisper, and most of her language was in technicolor. Her actions were much like those of a junior-aged boy. She paid little attention to her general appearance and at times was rather unladylike in her comportment.

Betty appeared one night at a meeting of the young adult fellowship in her church. She sat down and waited for the meeting to begin. The other members looked at her and then rolled their eyes at each other in mixed amusement and bewilderment. The two girls on either side of her suddenly recalled that they had unfinished business with persons on the opposite side of the circle. Betty was more persistent than dense. She followed them over to see what was so interesting. Everyone was just a little uneasy. This was totally unexpected and equally unwanted.

The meeting proceeded. One or two members made half-hearted attempts to include Betty in the conversation. The meeting ended without incident. The following week Betty was back, then the next week and the next. The group had about come to the conclusion that since the advisors were being of no help in finding a polite means to discourage her attendance they should tolerate her presence.

Then later in the year came an invitation to attend a joint meeting with another similar fellowship group at a nearby church. Guess who signed up first, and at that later meeting made a bigger show of herself than usual! That was too much . . . even for a church group!

It happened that Betty was absent the following week. The advisor arrived a few minutes late, but in time to hear the group trying to appoint someone to bear the tidings to Betty that her presence was no longer appreciated . . . all in a nice way, of course! Then the advisor shared with the group an edited report of what had already begun to happen because of their tolerance up to this point.

He had been in close touch all the while with Betty's social worker. That very week the worker had told Betty she no longer needed to come in to see her except on her own accord. She told the fellowship advisor

I don't need to see her. That group of yours is doing far more for her right now than I can. That's all she's talked about during her last appointments. Do you know this is the first group in which she's ever taken part that has refused to kick her out because of what she does? I don't know how you manage over there sometimes, because I do know how Betty behaves. Here . . . you might be interested in the report they sent me when she was released from the hospital.

Essentially, the report said that although Betty was definitely well enough to be home, she was not completely cured. Her problems would make problems for those responsible for her the rest of her life. Probably she would never be able to hold a job.

Enough of this was shared with the group to help them see that in their very reluctant presence a redemptive act had been taking place, and that they might even be a part of its continuation if they chose! This was the first time they as a group had had an experience of actually *being* the Church. They were coming to a new and deeper understanding of the meaning of genuine acceptance, and of the tremendous potential for Christian service they had together. They did go on, though at times that going got so rough that they looked for escape again.

Careful Planning Essential

That group had been unwillingly pushed into the experience with Betty. There had been no time for formal preparation. Things had to go on . . . with one difference . . . every plan and every activity had to have in it a place for Betty. That took some very careful work.

First it had to be determined what the role of the ministers would be. In that particular situation the associate minister was responsible for leadership of the Christian education program, the various youth work efforts and Junior Church, during the Sunday morning sermon hour. This continuing ministry, like any other, had to be anticipated and planned insofar as remained possible. In this situation where the beginnings were forced upon the congregation by Betty, several important measures had to be taken. Since these are quite essential, we ought to discuss them here and now.

In the first place, the two ministers had to come to a clear understanding of what such ministries as this would mean for them and for the church. It is quite likely that at some points efforts to work with fringe people can consume a lot of precious time. There had to be, therefore, acceptance of the possibility that at points this effort might demand the expenditure of what by normal standards would seem an inordinate amount of time . . . for the benefit of one or at best a very few persons. It would also create the need for a good deal of interpretation. Church treasurers and trustees might find it hard to justify putting so many eggs in a single basket.

There would be raised the whole question of potential disruptions of regular programs in church school classes, choirs and fellowship groups. Then there was the church image in the community. Smile if you will, but these are very real questions which were asked and which will be asked in your church if you attempt such ministries. You are hereby advised to have thought carefully about the answers before you begin.

The interpretation had to begin with the Board of Christian Education. Here were those who had responsibility for the total formal Christian education effort of the church. This had to be something worthy of their support. Interpretation could not be left to the ministers alone. These persons would be talking with teachers, leaders and parents, answering their questions and enlisting their help. They had to know the possibility that in the long run the effort might add dollars to the total Christian Education portion of the church budget.

Then there would need to be some sermons and special programs directed particularly to concerns about the Christian implications of relationships between persons. The ministers would have to make available in-service training opportunities for special orientation of teachers on such themes as "The Class Period as a Christian Laboratory," "Love and Discipline," "Teaching Materials or Persons?", and "Handling Difficult Moments Together." No church has the right to ask one to accept special responsibilities without first offering him special tools with which to do it and skills in using them. We shall say more of this later.

There were some basic principles everyone would have to remember, beginning with the ministers. Under no circumstances could this become a "Be-nice-to-Betty crusade." This ministry was to be with persons, not guinea pigs. In fact, it had to be the very same ministry shared with every other person. The differences would lie in the area of language difficulties such as those mentioned in the last chapter. The real problems, then, lay not with Betty or other "problem" people but with those who would be dealing with them. This meant that the ministers, and later the teachers and the other leaders would have to refresh themselves on some of the dynamics of group interaction and communication, the redemptive potential of meaningful inter-personal relationships, as well as some of the hurdles to be overcome if real progress was to be made. Thus without predicting specific actions, the ministers had to anticipate some of the reactions with which they and the congregation would probably have to deal.

In all likelihood some parents and even group members would be fearful of the contamination of the group, or at least its reputation, by the real involvement of persons who "really didn't fit." There were in fact some questions brought to the ministers about the reservations "some people" had about getting carried away with a pet theory. Extra interpretive work was necessary with the parents who didn't want their children "thrown in with delinquents or worse." As the weeks passed, this fear began slowly to subside. Actually, no group participant withdrew on this account, though for a while several were watching to see what the others would do, in good teenage fashion.

Then there was the matter of group prestige. It's one thing to have such unlovely persons in the church family and quite another to own to it before another group in the community! Temptations ran from discouraging the attendance of the persons in question to acting as if the group didn't really know them. (Incidentally, in the incident already mentioned it was rather a comfort to those thus disturbed to find the other group had also made a place for fringe persons in their circle!)

Both of the above worries were diminished with comparative ease as experience began proving them to have been unfounded. However, there were other higher hurdles. The idea of being a real neighbor within the fellowship had been quite appealing to the young people on the whole. Both pastors were proud of the efforts of the young people to put into practice the things they'd been learning about themselves and their potential as part of the redemptive fellowship of the church.

The other thing they would probably have to learn with some pain was that kindness is not always received in the same spirit. An outsider has to be careful. He is likely to take new kinds of experience in little doses and to test them carefully. If we can think back objectively, we have done this ourselves as newcomers. Usually we just wait and do our testing passively. In most instances questions like these go through our minds: "Why are they being nice to ME? Do they think I need charity? I wonder how much of this is for real. Maybe there's some angle here."

The outsider who has had few if any meaningful relationships with others may become quite uneasy when he feels others are getting too close to him. If he is one who acts out his feelings, in delinquent fashion, he may do his testing by doing unacceptable things to see if these people love stinkers as well as angels. If he can get them to pick up their marbles and go home he's proven they're phonies and at the same time saved himself considerable painful involvement.

One member of the gang to which this writer was assigned by the Boston Children's Service Association carried such testing to the point of jumping the wires and stealing the agency car while the group was visiting a zoo in the company of the worker. The first question asked of the worker after the incident was "S'pose we don't have no more club meetin's, huh?" When they were assured by the worker that it was up to them and not him, the succeeding meetings took on a noticeably different character. It's just a bit disconcerting to go out of one's way for someone else in love and then to receive a kick in the shins in return, but that's just the sort of thing that can happen as people try to build new relationships with hard-to-reach persons.

Still another lesson must more often be learned than taught in these kinds of circumstances. It is very normal to begin by planning what you can do *for* the individual who doesn't quite fit. There are things you want to do for him and perhaps things you can give him to make certain he knows of your love for him. These things can easily be done in a detached fashion without any personal involvement. Truthfully, this is a common tendency in early relationships of this nature. Yet, if anything real is to happen, people have to enter into meaningful relationships themselves—to give not things but themselves. No reasonable facsimiles will do! Persons have to be needed and wanted, and to have *their* particular talents used!

A fifteen-year-old boy, small for his age, but considerably larger than his junior and junior high choir mates began attending weekly Junior Choir rehearsals. He wore a leather jacket, complete with spangles, chewed gum incessantly, talked out of the side of his mouth, carried a doubled-up bicycle chain for "protection," and in short, was the very embodiment of what the other children had only seen in the movies or on television.

The first week he attended he began to act out. The leader quietly reminded him that probably things would go best if he kept things down to a dull roar. By the next week his behavior was right back at the point where it had left off. Again, and more firmly, he was warned that such behavior could not be tolerated. This worked for three whole weeks.

The fourth week the group was preparing to rehearse for a special Christmas program at the local television station. There were about thirty children to be ushered to the station on foot, a distance of three blocks, including crossings at two major intersections. Not one of the invited parents had arrived to help in the undertaking. As the hour approached, the two leaders became desperate. Finally one of them turned to Fred and pleaded, "Fred, you know how the smaller ones tear around. We'll have trouble if we don't keep track of them. Do you suppose you could help keep them in line?" "Sure thing! Hey!! D'jah hear what he said? Get in L-I-N-E!" Without a word the entire troupe lined up, hand in hand, two by two, and *stayed* that way until they arrived at the station!

The difference was clear in retrospect: This was the first time an adult had said anything to Fred but "Fred! Keep it down!" or "Fred! Stop that!" Instead someone said essentially "Fred, I need what you have to offer. Will you help me?"

That was the beginning of a long, painful but increasingly meaningful ministry to an entire *family*. Up to that point Fred had been perfectly welcome to come if he chose, and provided he behaved himself. He could even participate if he didn't get in the way. Yet, Fred and each of us wants something more than toleration in the group to which we belong. We want to be needed and therefore used . . . to know firsthand that we as persons and our talents are of value. We want to be asked to *play* on the team, rather than to watch. Nevertheless the step from one to the other is often a long one; one where again the pastor may be needed for development of insight and new skills. At all levels this implies a sort of involvement which is at first difficult.

A high school youth group became concerned one year about some sort of ministry with boys in their state boys' school. This was partly due to the fact that one of their members and his friend had recently been committed there. After conferences with the chaplain and the administrator of the institution, a plan was adopted for alternating programs once each month with the boys of a given cottage group.

The first month the chaplain brought the boys to the church in the school bus. Then the following month the fellowship group went out to the school. The first meeting was like a junior high dance. On one side of the meeting hall were all of the tongue-tied boys from the school. Facing them were the equally inarticulate church group members. Each was afraid to speak for fear of saying the wrong thing.

The second month the same thing occurred. After that each group held a caucus, and each decided to give it one more try, taking a great deal more initiative. Evidently they really wanted it to work, for that third meeting was deeply enjoyed by all. Driving back to the school, the chaplain overheard one of the boys say to his pal, "Gee, they made us feel like *people* again!" The mere provision of space and an occasion for meeting hadn't done the trick. Personal commitment and involvement had.

A concerned but inadequately prepared congregation in the suburbs of an eastern city learned that lesson the hard way. They wanted to influence the increasingly delinquent behavior of a gang of young people who counted as home territory the neighborhood about the church building. At considerable expense they created and equipped a teen canteen in the basement of the church. Then they invited the gang to join in its use. The third time the group wrecked the room the church wrote off the entire effort as a failure. The gift of facilities, the development of programs or the preachment of values are unlikely to be efficacious unless they are within a context of genuine personal involvement with those to be served.

This is both psychologically and theologically true. We ought to remember that it is possible to *dodge* that very sort of involvement by the giving of things rather than ourselves. No such substitute will deceive any of us for long if at all. Too often the line between gifts

and self-giving has been the outer boundary of the service of allegedly "concerned" persons. That sort of effort in the long run is nearly
always disappointing to all concerned. The pastor who would lead his
flock in growing ministries with outsiders should be supplying such a
perspective early in the planning of each venture to be undertaken.

Two other cautions ought to be shared with the congregation by
the pastor. The first has to do with the goal of the ministries which
are attempted by the church. Our over-concern with behavior, and
the easy assumption that church membership and good behavior are
about synonymous, together can lead us to establish unwise goals. It
may very well be that meaningful ministries with some fringe persons may never eventuate in church membership. What real business
have we to demand this? The Master did not speak to persons in
terms of church membership, but rather that wholeness of life which
is the root meaning of salvation. It's just possible that our ministries
with hard-to-reach persons may help them discover new fullness in
life without their ever becoming officially associated with the church.

It should be said immediately that this is in no way meant to deny
the desirability or the value of church membership. Rather it is to
remind us to guard against qualifying our ministries to any degree in
terms of the likelihood of the persons concerned applying for church
membership. To do so would be to give mute testimony to a lack of
the genuine involvement of ourselves about which we have just
spoken. Our purpose ought not to be the re-creation of persons in our
(institutional) image, but rather the bringing to light the already
existing image of God in a person.

Secondly, we ought to be sufficiently aware of how persons grow
and mature to realize that significant changes in one's life more often
than not take a great deal of time. Too many church programs operate as if their authors believed the things they did would have as
sudden and phenomenal results as the beans which overnight pro-
duced Jack's famous beanstalk. This writer will always remember the
following bit of conversation with a young man who as a child had
probably been labeled as a lost cause by his teachers:

Rich: By the way, I've got something to tell you. Maybe you'd
             better sit down first, though.

Minister: Okay, shoot.

Rich: Well, Jan and I have been talking about things up there where we're going to move. One of the first things we're going to do is find us a church.

Minister: Well, that *is* good. . . .

Rich: Wait a minute, I'm not finished! . . . You remember what a stinker I always was while I was in high school?

Minister: Uh-huh.

Rich: Well, it went back a long way before that, too. You know, I don't remember a thing you or any of the rest tried to teach me, but one thing *did* stick. Not one of you ever kicked me out. I had it comin' lots of times, but nobody did it. You don't know what that meant all that time. I guess I didn't myself, really. But we've been talking it over. You know what we want to do?

Minister: I begin to get an idea.

Rich: We both want to see if they'll let us teach in the Sunday school. I don't know whether I'd be any good at it, but I'd like to give it a turn. I figure if I could get to some kid and do for him what you people did for me it wouldn't be a complete waste of time. Jan feels the same. We both want to try it.

Here was one who grew up in the church . . . on the outside. Not until he was a young husband did the frustrating work with him begin to pay off, long after most had lost hope.

Members of the youth group which attempted a ministry with boys at the state school cherished the hope that two of the boys in particular would, as a result of their work, return to the group when they were released. One boy was a member and everyone wanted him to continue to feel himself a part of the group regardless of his past actions and subsequent commitment. Yet, upon release, neither he nor his friend showed up at fellowship meetings. The other members were both disappointed and disillusioned.

However, about two years later, the other young man and his wife brought their first child before the church for dedication. In the front pew sat his buddy and their two families. And everyone was surprised! They had been as ready to accept failure as success—overnight. It had not occurred to them that perhaps the fruits of their labors might not be realized until those boys as parents someday attempted to introduce their children to what they had known briefly as young persons through that particular fellowship group.

Not infrequently it takes that long for miracles to happen. In our hurrying world that may seem too long. Once again, that's where a pastor can be of great help. His under-shepherds may very naturally look for early and clear indications that their efforts have been "successful." His understanding of persons and his long experience will be invaluable in tempering the expectations of his overly eager lay ministers.

Perhaps one important reminder is in order at this point. The Samaritan neighbor, upon finding the wounded man went right about administering first aid. Jesus' story doesn't say that he fidgeted about, talking about the weather or the championship camel races being held that day in Jerusalem. It does not say that he tried to get the man's mind off pain by drawing his attention to everything else but the real problem. Instead he began to treat the wounds.

Let us not delude ourselves. Those groups, as well as individuals, which seek to minister to outsiders in their midst may sometimes be wounded and hurt in the process. That is not the time to smile sweetly and act as if it were not so! Yet, our tendency to maintain harmony-at-any-cost within the church frequently leads us to do just that. When difficulties arise, we tend to ignore them, childishly hoping they'll go away. Meanwhile, without benefit of communication, hurt feelings and misunderstandings multiply and deepen. When enough steam has been generated, the lid blows off, and those who are nearby are seriously injured. Then there may not be enough left of previous relationships to repair.

How tragically often it is that at the point where persons differ they separate! That happens in the church as often as elsewhere. Yet the church is the place where, because of the unity we have in Christ, we ought rather to draw closer together to share those specific differences.

Our unity does not demand uniformity. In fact, genuine unity can best be seen in the midst of diversity. We can and should accept each other regardless of whether we agree on all matters. However, most social groups behave as if they did not really believe there was anything for two persons in disagreement to do but separate. Jesus advised the man who had something against his brother to go to his brother and get it straightened out, then he would be ready for worship. (Matt. 5:23–24)

If we are to *be* the Church "at church" we can't walk away from the problems that confront us there. A steady diet of sweetness and light without genuine encounter can and not infrequently does leave a group spiritually flabby. When a person stands forth in his group, posing problems of communication and relationships, we dare not, for love of comfort, leave him alone or at the mercy of the group he has disturbed. To do so is to say that although we preach the individual worth of each person as a child of God, we would rather leave him to wrestle alone with his problems than to risk a disturbance in the group.

It is precisely at such points in their experience that many groups grow most noticeably. There is nothing wrong with disagreement or frustration or anger. They are perfectly natural experiences. Nevertheless, the frenetic effort to insure tranquility in our groups leads people to think that to disagree, to feel frustrated or to become angry is wrong.

We've all been part of groups where there was positively no room for such reactions. Probably this is more true of church groups than any others. What really happens is that we take our grievances and misunderstandings away with us to others who we know share our feelings. These groups within the group wage guerilla battles with each other, which are intensified by the lack of communication which has resulted from their drawing apart in the first place. This is really little more sophisticated than the once-common resort to dueling, and in many instances the two measures are on a par in terms of their tragic consequences.

When I as a group member express an idea contrary to those of the rest of the group, I want my idea to be honored by serious group consideration whether anyone agrees with me or not. Otherwise, how can I be sure that my acceptance in the group doesn't really depend on being on the right side or behaving in the prescribed manner? If that is so, just how significant is the "love" and "acceptance" these Christians proclaim? If I am important, as these churchmen say, then it seems someone ought to take me seriously as a person. I need to know that others are genuinely aware of my presence when I'm around, that they note my absence or early leaving, that they listen to what I have to say. Then their preaching will begin to make sense.

One outsider began attending the weekly meetings of a church youth fellowship group. In matters of decision-making, the group overlooked him from the first. He countered by being "against" everything that was decided. Twice the members became so frustrated by this reaction that they asked the leader *in the presence of the boy* to make him leave because he was creating such a disturbance.

Only after long and patient efforts to encourage utilization of *every* contribution made to the group did they begin to accept him and thus take his ideas seriously. As this happened he found less and less need to assert himself. It was right at the point of conflict that the members grew most. Not a few times the planned program was delayed or even put aside to focus upon tense relationships.

Who is to say who benefitted most by the refusal of the leader to throw someone out because his behavior wasn't acceptable? Was it the offender or those others who were thereby assured that no matter what they did *they* would never be dismissed themselves at the point where their behavior might get out of bounds? They knew from then on *because they had seen it happen* and then right there they had talked about what they had just seen.

This was vividly illustrated in a novel way shortly after someone we'll call George Anderson became advisor to a strong-willed high school age church youth group. His predecessor had been extremely popular with the group. Even when George arrived, the group was still bemoaning the loss of their former leader. This, coupled with the different ways in which George looked at some things, brought forth a good deal of early resentment toward him as leader. Realizing this, he began, as soon as the group was ready, helping them to discuss and slowly discover the real roots of their very natural reactions. This was done in the midst of regular group sessions. Gradually, attitudes mellowed and then became strongly positive.

A time came three years later when George announced that he would be leaving soon to begin a new chapter in his ministry. Immediately it was evident that the same cycle was likely to recur unless preventive measures were taken. He spent a good deal of time talking with those who had since become members of the youth fellowship, helping them to see how natural it would be to measure his successor by him, and to reject the newcomer since he wouldn't and couldn't be George.

George began calling on some of the older youths who had earlier rejected him. He talked with them and their parents, and together they planned ways to help their younger brothers and sisters meet the challenge of accepting a new leader. Those most committed to the effort were the same ones who had given George the most difficulty when he had first arrived. With his help they had faced that situation *right in the midst of their group meetings.*

They were convinced now that the rejection of *any* person in the Church or elsewhere was contrary to the intent of the Christian Good News. In the remaining two months of George's ministry there that group and their older brothers and sisters went a long way toward assuring the genuine acceptance of *any* newcomer to the fellowship. It wouldn't have happened and they themselves would have been deprived of opportunities for future ministries together if George had not encouraged the young people to face directly and on the spot the problems with which they were actually wrestling.

Perhaps this gives a sufficient indication of the indispensable role to be played by the pastor in any ministries with hard-to-reach persons within the church. We have by no means covered the entire range of his responsibilities. In fact, the reader may already wonder what has happened to the popular concern with pastoral counseling. The omission, if that is what it is, has not been accidental.

In the first place, pastors frequently find that direct counseling relationships with hard-to-reach young people must be preceded by other, less formal ministries. In fact, the pastor may never counsel directly with some of those persons. Moreover, it often happens that those first efforts are carried forward by lay people. This is not to say that a pastor's ministry of counseling picks up where lay programs leave off. It should have been clear by this time that the pastor's ministry really begins in the guidance and encouragement of those who may first make contact with outsiders.

Secondly, if it is indeed true that a pastor is not himself the only minister of his congregation, but rather, that he leads members in ministries which are theirs together, then the things which have been said here so far ought to apply equally to his special ministry of counseling.

Thus in a very deep sense we have been talking all along about the *pastor's* ministry with hard-to-reach youth. Those things which are fundamental to his direct pastoral relationships with hard-to-reach persons must characterize the efforts of the whole Church in its total witness for Christ with outsiders. To put it another way, these tools and skills will have to be part of his professional equipment and his work before they can be applied to the efforts of lay people in their frequent early opportunities to work meaningfully with unrelated persons.

What About Comparable Ministries Outside?

So far, we have been speaking of the Church's ministry with outsiders who have somehow gravitated to the fringes of existing church groups and programs. However, we are all aware of the fact that there are many unrelated persons who never get that close to a church. We may wait inside the doors of the church forever, and discover that many refuse to cross the threshold. Does this mean that since they have not flocked to us to receive what we have offered, that we have at least discharged our responsibility? Not a few of us have been tempted to hide behind that pious excuse.

A problem something like this has been increasingly disturbing social work agencies in this country. Some persons have rather deep-seated fears or antagonistic feelings about institutions of any sort. Some refuse to go to a hospital until a critical emergency is reached. Others indicate by the poor attendance records of their children that they have little use for schools. Social workers are frustrated beyond words by those who don't follow instructions or keep appointments. Still others, though deeply religious, want little if anything to do with an organized church.

Of course, the schools have the legal means to deal with each child until the age of sixteen. Nevertheless, without solid motivation on the part of the children, there are severe limits upon what can be done in the carefully structured atmosphere of the school.

It boils down to this: if unreached persons are to be reached, something in addition to standard institutional efforts will have to be employed. Perhaps we can appropriate for ourselves the lesson Mohammed is said to have learned—if unrelated persons will not come to us, and if we are serious about our desire to minister with them, then we must go *to them.*

This suggests definitely aggressive procedures. It is a strange thing that though we speak often of the Church militant we seldom seem to have incorporated in that thinking aggressive, personal efforts to reach out after people. Rather, we tend to limit the concept of militancy outside the Church to formal crusades for this or against that.

Possibly this is because we have not put into action the idea that a church dispersed is still the Church. Consequently, when this has been so, we have assumed that the work of the Church was only done when its members were gathered for action, that the work of the Church was merely church-work. We know better than this, but many of us forget when we are apart in our own little worlds. We ask the rhetorical question, "What can *I* do?" and, feeling that the obstacles before us as individuals are insurmountable, shrug our shoulders and search for other fields to harvest. However, this is exactly where some dynamic ministries can and must take place if our total ministries with unreached persons are to be genuinely effective.

Naturally, the opportunities for dealing directly with unreached persons outside institutional structures cannot be programmed precisely. They come largely without warning. All the same, a developed sensitivity to this sort of need can turn up undreamed-of possibilities.

This writer was called to the staff of the Council of Churches of Evansville, Indiana, to help develop lay ministries with emotionally disturbed and delinquent young people. This was a pilot venture, in the sense that its focus was upon the potential ministries of laymen. A committee of sixteen men from four churches had launched the venture after more than two years of wrestling with a strong but undefined sense of mission with disturbed and delinquent children. Several had had one-to-one relationships with boys in trouble, and their varied experiences had only made them sure that with help they should be capable of meaningful relationships with these children.

Numerous openings have developed. First of all, to pave the way for helpful relationships with delinquent boys and girls, it was decided to ask permission to provide a qualified Church representative at the weekly hearings in Juvenile Court. That responsibility, when approved, went to the new staff person. Its purpose was to make possible a bridge between the work of the court and that of the Church.

Most of the children who come before the juvenile authorities because of their delinquent acts, and who have had some touch with a church, "forget" to tell their pastors of their referral to court. However, this representation at the court makes it possible, where advisable, to make available the resources of the church in helping the young person find himself. This means that on a professional basis and in a confidential manner the pastor of the church in question can be alerted to the possibility of helping.

That first involves the suggestion that the pastor get in touch with the court probation officer to plan a coordinated approach to the boy or girl involved. Then the pastor in turn may quietly enlist the services of a dependable and understanding layman for the major touch with that young person. Perhaps it is a Scout leader, a teacher or just a conscientious fellow churchman. Without divulging the details of the offense committed the pastor can guide the layman in his dealings with the young person in ways he and the court officer have felt would be most appropriate.

In other situations there appears to have been no previous church association. Again if it seems appropriate, an unchurched young offender can be referred to a church in the vicinity of his home. That is of course an arbitrary decision to make, and in practice depends upon such factors as the character of the youngster's attitudes and behavior, the observed or apparent reactions of the church and the pastor toward young or other offenders, and the pastor's specific training and experience for such a ministry.

Such decisions are as subjective as they are arbitrary. Yet experience indicates that this is both possible and necessary. An unaccepting group of boys and girls, a general judgmental attitude on the part of a congregation or the lack of pertinent experience and/or training; any or all of these may make a referral inadvisable, at least for the present.

Sometimes the chance for a referral arises before a delinquency petition is filed with the court. A lady returned to her home after chatting with a neighbor, to find her paper-boy in her kitchen. When she attempted to pay him, she discovered he had just rifled her purse. Shortly afterward she called her pastor, because, she said, she was not interested in punishment but in being of real help. Her pastor in turn called the Council advisor for guidance.

The boy had spasmodically attended a church other than her own. She realized that the solution was certainly not to lure him from his church to hers. Eventually, a conference was arranged for her, the boy's pastor and the Council's advisor, to make plans for a team approach to the developing needs of the boy. Each projected his anticipated role in the over-all strategy, the one as pastor and the other as a continuing customer. As it turned out, the boy's behavior erupted again before the plan could be put to work, the boy lost his paper route and his pastor went to another church. Nevertheless, the process is indicative of the way the Church can be instrumental in dealing with a hard-to-reach young person.

Not long after that a series of violent delinquent acts were committed by unsupervised and unrelated boys in various parts of the community. The temptation was strong among several churchmen to set out on a crusade to correct the situation. Instead, a meeting was called to try to determine the real nature of the problems involved. Invited to that gathering were law enforcement officers, representatives of the schools, courts, housing authority, the recreation commission, PTA and other churches.

For the better part of two years this group worked on the problem, which seemed to center about a lack of touch and of supervision of older teenage children. At last, it was decided to begin a cooperative pilot effort to see if a special approach might reach otherwise unreached older boys.

The vehicle for the effort was to be a relatively unstructured program of "more virile" athletics, i.e. opportunities for instruction in body building through weight-lifting, boxing and wrestling. It was not to be a church project as such, but rather a community venture in which churchmen could play a very important role. In part that was done by the persons who contributed the funds for the operation of the project and the purchase of equipment. A former All-America football player who starred under Knute Rockne, "Jumpin' Joe" Savoldi, agreed to be the instructor.

The churches recruited and trained a group of church laymen to serve each Thursday night as adult companions and advisors to the boys as they worked out. The help of the police department and the schools was solicited in order to determine whom to approach as potential participants in the program. A churchman called personally on boys known to be leaders of unreached groups.

At the end of the school year, nearly one hundred boys had registered with the athletic club the boys later formed. About twenty-five had earned a club shirt by achieving a minimum of five consecutive weekly meetings without an absence. Over ten percent of the boys were in court during the period. This was partial evidence that the plan had provided a means for touch with the very persons about whom the whole effort was focused. The only question being asked at this point was "Can we reach unreached boys by this means?"

For our present concerns, the significant thing here was the involvement of dedicated church laymen in a project of real religious significance which had no "religious" labels. Here were ministers whose sermons happened. Here were Christians, Negro and white, Catholic and Protestant, helping boys take their first steps toward the sort of relationships which are a manifestation of the religious truth that all of us are brothers, one of another. That kind of opening for volunteer help, under supervision, is more often available in communities than resident churchmen realize!

Of course, two things are helpful in uncovering and developing such opportunities. The one is a strong relationship of churches to community agencies and other resource groups. Secondly, that very relationship and the actual planning to meet identified need on the part of churches seems to function most efficiently when there exists in the community some sort of cooperative church organization, such as a local council of churches. This has certainly been true of the situations with which this writer has been familiar.

For example, it is a fact that when a community has such a resource, agency leaders often turn to it for the recommendation of persons to fill positions of leadership within their respective programs. Thus, local council executives are not infrequently asked to suggest the names of persons to work in volunteer programs, to serve as officers or board members of agencies. In many instances this affords the opportunity to help provide and extend services to the very persons with whom we are here concerned. A conscientious, trained layman may be worth much more than his weight in gold to a school board, a juvenile court advisory committee, a legislative advisory group, yes, even a political action group. These groups are always engaged in services with people which continue where lay efforts leave off.

A third factor is essential to any volunteer team work on community problems. Good intentions just aren't enough! Many are the professionals who have cringed inwardly when offered help by a concerned but uninformed volunteer. If churches encourage the involvement of church people in volunteer work on community problems, there should be some training done by the church, and with the help of available resource people from the community. In these matters, as with so many, a little knowledge, unassimilated and without benefit of tempering guidance, can be a dangerous thing.

Here then is a further indication of the potential role of the local pastor in preparing his parishioners for truly effective Christian witnessing in extra-church community settings. A pastor ought to be rather familiar with how a community lives and functions. Few people seem to appreciate the significance of this sort of information. Thus, when stirred up to the point of action, they are very upset to find that certain facts of community living must govern that action. It can be terribly disconcerting for a group seeking an appropriation of public funds for a very worthy cause to discover that budgetary requests must be made at least six months before the money, if approved, can become available. Should the group run past that deadline, or have their request denied, as much as eighteen months will probably have to elapse before there is another possibility of having money available for their cherished project. Sometimes it takes two or three turns around in as many years to receive approval of such requests. Then they may wonder "Why should it take so long for something *this* important?" The pastor who from the beginning acquaints his people with some of these facts of life in a community will do much to effectively equip them for worthwhile efforts.

These same people may be in danger of disillusionment if they are not helped to understand how decisions are made in any community, even in that of a family. Church people seem to have developed a common idea that compromise is an evil, inglorious thing. Actually, it is a common experience in all of life. Any group which faces its problems has to become involved in compromises. Yet when that happens at the level of community decisions or of legislative action, people think that it is wrong.

Parents may suggest fingerpainting for the child who is most happy smearing less desirable materials on things and himself. The boy who will never make the school's varsity football squad becomes the best manager the team ever had. Dad's fancy is caught by the sleek lines and special equipment on a custom-built, expensive car. Mother is more practical and insists on a compact. They buy something in between the two.

Yet when a city councilman votes against a reform proposal and instead supports a compromise measure, he is immediately castigated as a mealy-mouthed, unprincipled or even an evil man. When a legislator trades his backing of one bill for a promise of support on another, many quickly chalk this up to dirty politicking. In a very real sense this may amount to the establishment of priorities which the community ought to have taken responsibility for setting earlier. Then, too, it may actually reflect priorities which have in fact already been agreed upon back home.

The point is that compromise is not necessarily the bad thing so many Christian people assume it to be. You as a pastor doubtless have in mind some things in the life of your church which you would like to see changed. There are probably more of them than it would be humanly possible to alter today. You will not bring them all up today nor will you insist that they all must be adjusted tomorrow. That means that tonight you will be abiding by some situations of which you heartily disapprove. Won't you be compromising your position on those matters, pastor? Six months from today you will probably be working on some of the items of your present agenda. You will perhaps be saying "This congregation just isn't ready for this sort of experience yet," and you'll probably be right. *Your* conscience may even be calling you to task for compromising.

The truth is that compromise is not inherently wrong. Furthermore, in the long run, it is often a necessary part of growth and maturity. However, you as a pastor will find many of your people will need a lot of patient help to learn this lesson with which you have yourself struggled. Until they have mastered it, their role in decision-making processes may be both frustrated and frustrating. We could continue, but hopefully, the stage has been set.

We began this chapter by saying that its intent was to be more specific. Obviously that was not the promise of a set of precise measures to be employed in every situation we may encounter in the course of the ministries we have been contemplating. Even physical maladies are subject to too many complications to warrant blanket rules of treatment for them all. Modern studies of psychosomatic relationships emphasize the complexity of persons as a whole.

Thus the effort here has been rather to focus our attention on some particular demands placed upon those of us, and pastors particularly, who would minister for Christ with hard-to-reach young persons. We've noted that the best place for beginning is with those outsiders who hover about the fringes of our regular church groups. It was pointed out that even mere toleration can sometimes have healing effects.

Considerable attention was given to the need for careful preparation of people anticipating ministries with persons who don't fit. These things don't just happen. Wise leadership and sustaining supervision are especially important in this sort of endeavor. Most often, this is the place where the pastor's relationship begins or is even fully realized. We must realize that this is an area where misunderstandings can abound and valid ministries may be aborted if there is a lack of interpretation.

It may well be that long before a minister is sought out for direct pastoral help lay persons in his congregation have been ministering to the one in question. In truth, those prior ministries may have actually brought the person to the pastor. That merely underlines the fact that really significant ministries with any persons are much more than a few specific things we do or say; more nearly, they are the reflections of ongoing total relationships. It is a pastor's high privilege and responsibility to help people discover their created relationships to each other and the tremendous potential for healing in the fulfillment of those ties.

Another way of saying this is that the pastor's role, especially in these ministries, may most often be a ministry with (lay) ministers. That viewpoint is biblically sound and certainly in keeping with a major segment of Christian tradition. It means that special thought and effort must be given to training teachers and other leaders for dealing effectively with the special needs of unreached persons. In most instances that must come from the pastor. He will often be the one who must supply and help maintain the perspectives of basic purpose of involvement through self giving, patient persistence in the face of frustration and even rejection, of the genuine acceptance of persons without reference to their behavior and of a realistic confrontation of actual problems as they occur. Thus it appears that the pastoral ministry, where hard-to-reach persons are the focus of concern, may involve more counseling with those who in turn work with such persons than direct personal touch with those outsiders.

We said further that the same truths apply to extra-church, community ventures and relationships. Thus the pastor's role as minister of ministers must also include preparation for participation in efforts which may not always be clearly identifiable religiously. It may include assistance in acclimatization to procedures and manners of doing things that are very difficult to accept. We said it might even involve the counsel to occasionally accept such things as compromise or interminable waiting and endless campaigning for changes.

All of this still leaves only partially answered a question which was raised earlier and deserves further attention: "Why, if we have not yet done all there is to be done with those we have begun to reach, should we devote so much attention to the hard-to-reach?" Perhaps if we wrestle with this challenge a bit more we shall come up with an over-arching perspective for all that has been said here. Let's turn back, now, to the Church, whose ministries with hard-to-reach young people have been our concern in this book.

CHAPTER EIGHT

MEANWHILE, BACK At The CHURCH . . .

This book is about the Church's ministry with hard-to-reach persons. What meaning have the things we have been saying for the continuing life of the Church? What could we expect if we actually put some of these ideas into practice?

We have been exploring avenues for ministries which would be costly in many respects. It has been emphasized that many of the efforts discussed could consume a seemingly disproportionate share of the available time of both individuals and congregations. We have reminded ourselves that considerable language study is a must for meaningful communication with hard-to-reach young people. We've been cautioned not to look for early "results," and not to be too surprised if our first rewards are sore toes and barked shins.

The preceding chapter began with an exhortation to make a beginning right in the midst of the ongoing program of the church! With little more and often considerably less than an hour's time for church group meetings, what would be left for work with the "regular" or "normal" persons? Isn't the author, in his enthusiasm for the subject, suggesting that the church abandon its responsibility for the many in order to better serve the few?

The answer is no. However, it must be remembered that our Lord spoke often of God's great concern about the lost. He once said, "If a man has a hundred sheep and one of them has gone astray, does he not leave the ninety-nine on the hills and go in search of the one that went astray? . . . So it is not the will of my Father . . . that one of these little ones should perish." (Matt. 18:12ff). Then again he said "I have other sheep that are not of this fold; I must bring them also . . . So there will be one flock, one shepherd." (John 10:16). Perhaps, then, that alternative is not all wrong.

It is tempting here to rely entirely for an answer upon these passages and those in the Book of Acts dealing with the discovery by early Christians that the Good News is for all men for all time. However, this could lead us to assume something we have already said is not necessarily true. It would encourage one to infer that those who already have had touch with the Church are safely within its fold. We spent the first portion of the last chapter on the problems of effectively ministering with the unreached *in the church*. Actually, then, the above passages might be used to support a concentration of effort *within* the church and even among the "regulars." These separate texts and the message behind them do not tell the full story.

There is a more fundamental matter involved here. It is a lesson about which very little has been said so far. That is partly due to the fact that it is usually "caught" rather than "taught." We are speaking of the *tremendous potential for spiritual growth and new maturity of the individuals, groups and congregations who enter upon such ministries.*

Few of us can quickly recognize genuine growth in ourselves. This is sometimes partly due to the fact that real growth is often a painful process. This is not to say that all pain is an indication of growth. Some well-intentioned but poorly prepared groups have experienced real pain in their efforts to "be nice to the unfortunates and the bad-actors" without growing at all. Growth in the midst of unpleasant or hurting experiences is often obscured by the pain involved. Particularly, if we have been unable to do away with the discomfort of the situation it is hard to see that we have made progress. Yet the real test of growth in such circumstances may more often be the question "Have we improved our ability to cope with that pain while proceeding in these ministries?"

Incidentally, there is an indication here that the minister's work is not yet done. If it is as difficult as we have said to recognize growth in ourselves, we shall probably need some help to do so, from time to time. Very likely our pastor can help us discover what has been going on while we have been focusing our attention upon "outsiders." Just possibly, God's work with persons has not been limited to our piddling efforts with others! It may not be entirely accurate to say as we often do that "God has no hands but ours." . . . perhaps He has been doing some great thing with us while we have been devoting our efforts to the "hard-to-reach."

Another reason for our difficulty in recognizing growth in ourselves is the usual slow rate of such progress. This was noted in both the fifth and seventh chapters in speaking of work with unreached persons. Well, because we are persons, too, the same truth applies to us. We seldom are aware of the tangible physical changes in our bodies until we try to purchase a new dress or suit. Much less evident and perhaps even slower are the changes which come in our personalities and spiritual maturity. Not infrequently, when those changes are pointed out by others, we are prone to say "Really? I guess I hadn't noticed."

Then too, we seldom spend much time talking to others about growth we have recognized in ourselves. Possibly that is because in such matters we don't like to recall the fact that we were once comparatively immature and childish. The thing to remember is that although we may have difficulty in recognizing it, it is very likely that in the course of the ministries we have been considering *we* may be the ones who have profited most!

It seems to this writer that this is best appreciated in retrospect. Certainly if we launch our efforts with great anticipations of self improvement we are bound to begin looking almost from the first for "results" or at least side benefits in ourselves. In terms of the economy of our attention this can only divide our concerns and thus detract from the ministry we have originally espoused. Furthermore, the promise of personal growth benefits can lead us to gear what we do by the progressive changes we see in ourselves. To do that is to become guilty of the prostitution of our announced intentions. If my efforts to minister with my unreached brother are more basically an effort to improve myself, then to that degree I am using him for my own ends, and that is sinful. My brother is to be loved, not used.

Nevertheless, when a pastor encourages people to undertake ministries with hard-to-reach persons he ought to be aware of the great promise in that pursuit for the spiritual growth of those "reachers." He may even need to share with some of the leaders of his congregation some indication of that potential. Better, however, that the rest should be helped later to look back and recognize what has indeed happened while they have been busy serving each other.

Nothing has been said yet by way of illustration of the likely growth of the "reachers" which we have been assuming. A further look at some of the experiences previously mentioned in this book may be worthwhile.

When persons become intimately involved with each other they nearly always do so at the cost of some prejudices and preconceived ideas about each other and themselves. The shattering of such ideas is sometimes painful and frightening. At the same time this sort of discovery is a fair gauge of insight and of maturity, and a means of liberation for greater service. The reader's attention is called to the tenth chapter of the Book of the Acts of the Apostles in the New Testament. Peter's horizons had been sharply limited by those religious traditions of the Jews which affected their relationships with the rest of the world. According to all that Peter had learned from childhood Cornelius and his household were just not in line to receive the visitation of God's Holy Spirit. It was even against the law for Peter to have anything to do with such people. They were not Jews; not among the chosen. Yet God brought Peter to the realization that "God is no respecter of persons." That was not easy for Peter to accept and a source of even greater difficulty for those remaining in the church at Jerusalem. It was as these early Jewish Christians accepted this startling fact that the evangelization work of the church really got off the ground.

Those who accept calls to minister with people in conflict are likely to be similarly shaken by some of the discoveries they make. It's not at first comforting to know that those whom society treats as black sheep are terribly like the rest of us. We'd rather find in them constitutional peculiarities to substantiate our assumption that there are basic differences between us. Yet these people *do* things which are unallowable and which we have great difficulty understanding. How often good church people, hearing of a delinquent act committed by a young person, ask in bewilderment, "*What* would make a girl *do* a thing like that?" Of course, the real answer is "The same sorts of things which might bring any of us to commit a comparable or even a worse offense." This writer has not a few times wondered if, given the same sort of conditions over a period of time, he would have kept from delinquent behavior as long as some of the children he has seen in court.

Those of us who deal closely with troubled persons must first make the existential discovery that these people like us, are God's children every bit as much as we. They are those for whom Christ died. We say this glibly every Sunday, but usually approach such persons in a manner which clearly says otherwise. Gradually it begins to dawn on us, if we survive the inevitable testing, that these boys and girls are actually searching for the same things in life which we are finding in the church community. The fact that they look for meaning in the wrong places and in unproductive relationships is actually proof of this, though we seldom recognize it as such.[1] Once this is discovered we add a third dimension to our potential for real service.

Questions by church people about the "success" of work done with the gang of delinquent boys mentioned in the preceding chapter helped the worker appreciate what had really been happening. In spite of some advantageous graduate training, the worker had at first seriously wondered how to cope with the strange unacceptable behavior of the boys. Their actions were so blatantly offensive that they tended to distract his attention. He knew intellectually that this was in part the testing of his actual acceptance. Looking back, and recalling his supervisor's counsel, the worker began to understand that his most important assignment had been the establishment of meaningful relationships, rather than a transformation of behavior. He discovered that his concern for them as persons had been his real credentials. He hadn't needed any excuse or gimmick. (The gimmicks would actually have been rejected for being just that!) And, wonder of wonders, there had begun to appear some significant changes in the behavior patterns of the boys!

This was a group of individuals, mainly. Only in the case of an impending "jam" would they draw together, and then only for strength in the fight. In most other matters it was every man for himself. At the beginning, when a (usually stolen) candy bar was pulled out of one's pocket, a piece was torn off and the remainder put quickly back in the pocket before anyone else got his hands on it. Eight months later the procedure had been partially altered. Now when the candy bar (still stolen) came out of the pocket, noses were counted and then the owner would announce "Awright! Y'each get a half a piece, 'n' pass it AROUN'!" No, the worker had not been successful in curbing all the unacceptable behavior of the boys. However, he had learned firsthand that much of that behavior was a

[1] See again pp. 109 and 110, Chap. Six.

function of poor or non-existing relationships and that those needed attention first. These were the very fundamentals which are the concern of the Holy Scriptures and of the Church. He had been helping these boys to begin to discover their true, God-given identity. They had begun acting like the brothers they were, even in the use of their stolen candy! Incidentally, that experience taught him a lot about real essentials in his work with a church youth fellowship on Sundays! The author is in a good position to know about all this for he was the worker.

The older youth fellowship group and the junior choir grew in miraculous, though slow fashion in their experiences with Betty and Fred. They had all been carefully taught that because of God's wonderful love for all His children, they ought to love everyone. They knew that every person was their neighbor. They regularly recited prayers for all the people of the world. It had been easy. Generally speaking, the member of their groups had been very like themselves—lovable persons. To love fellow members had not been difficult. Their middle-class interests, comfortable economic status, and their racial and cultural uniformity had thus far deprived them of the sort of encounters which might have tested and brought new significance to these truths they had so easily owned.

Then came persons to their groups who just didn't fit the picture. Their presence disrupted the usual smooth patterns of operation. The newcomers were resented. Everything about them was unlovely and unlovable. That was where the rub came. It was clear that the leaders were acting as if these persons, too, were worthy of being loved. Of course "everybody" would have to include them, but *these* people . . . ?

Never before had it occurred to these church young people that loving one's neighbor might someday mean loving an unlovely person. They even began to look more critically at what they had assumed were relationships of love with one another. They found some of those ties dependent in part on their conformity to the pattern of the group. Gradually there came a new depth to their relationships. For the first time some of the members found themselves beginning to experience things they had only talked about before, things like genuine acceptance and forgiveness and the redemptive nature of the Church. They had been role playing—for real. It's doubtful that any alternative effort could have as effectively helped these young Christians to grow.

These young people had been told that they were the Church, and they had agreed to the idea. Yet this had been so little evidenced in the actual life of that church that the concept had been largely forgotten. They had heard of the priesthood of all believers and could probably have even written passable themes on the subject. Nevertheless it had never before occurred to them that they themselves might truly become the Church in their brief experiences together. The older group just could not believe that they had already been part of a healing ministry with one of their own number.

A great deal of value is placed today upon laboratory training in Christian education. In a laboratory school one has the opportunity to observe and often to be part of the things he is learning. We still tend to conduct programs of Christian education as if their only purpose was the transfer of religious information from teacher to pupil. Teacher training institutes and our denominational literature say differently, but their words are largely ignored in local church schools.

Only infrequently do professional Christian educators call attention to the fact that regular church school classes, fellowship groups, choirs and circles can be excellent laboratories for dynamic Christian learning and genuine personal growth. This is so, whether one believes it or not. Children are quick to see whether or not the things they are told match with the way they are received by a teacher or leader. Moreover, it is what *happens* that registers with them in their group experiences, just as Rich so clearly indicated.

Really, this book has been saying nothing new. It has not been advocating the scrapping of present church programs or personal dealings with young people. It has not called for the abandonment of our regular group members in order to spend our entire efforts with the few who don't quite belong or those who are totally unrelated.

We ought to have been reminded by the early chapters that hard-to-reach people are, after all, persons, that they are strangely like us, that they have the same basic needs as we. The means of communication with such persons may vary, but the ministry is essentially the one Christians have been proclaiming from the beginning.

We need to be aware of the true potential of our normal church group experiences to speak effectively for Christ to those who hover on the fringes of those circles. To the degree we become involved in such relationships we shall very likely be maturing spiritually more than we know. Perhaps thereby we shall understand what it means to be the Church more fully than ever before. Furthermore, on the basis of such experiences, we shall be prepared for meeting similar sorts of challenges out where we live in the world. It can happen right here and any one of us can be a part of it.

You who are a pastor will be the key to these discoveries and the enlarged ministries toward which they point. Yours will be the privilege of leading people into the laboratories of your church. You will be able to help them experience and share firsthand what they have been often told. You may well be equipping them to minister to outsiders with whom you'll never have a direct pastoral relationship. In short, you may be the catalytic agent which in your church laboratories enables many lay persons to minister effectively to the needs of persons we would have heretofore spoken of as the hard-to-reach.

BIBLIOGRAPHY

I. Adolescent Development.

BLAIR, ARTHUR W. and WILLIAM H. BURTON. *The Growth and Development of the Pre-Adolescent*. New York: Appleton-Century-Crofts, Inc., 1951. Here is a rare concentration upon the phases of psychological development which are usually summarily covered with the cloak of adolescence. This affords a keener appreciation of processes which lead into adolescence.

BLOS, PETER. *The Adolescent Personality*. New York: Appleton-Century-Crofts, Inc., 1941. A solid treatment of the topic by a respected authority.

COLEMAN, JAMES S. *The Adolescent Society*. New York: The Free Press of Glencoe, 1961. A study of the world of the modern adolescent as it is to be discovered in the setting of the high school, which is at its heart. Based on research conducted in ten high schools. Very little else is written on this important subject.

EISSLER, R. S. and others, editors. *The Psychoanalytic Study of the Child*. This series, now composed of 18 yearbooks, features a collection of papers by recognized leaders in its field. Although admittedly rather technical in content, this is an extremely valuable resource about which to know.

FRANK, ANNE. *Anne Frank: Diary of a Young Girl*. Translator: B. M. Mooyaart. New York: The Modern Library, 1952. This is a classic, poignant and insightful self-portrait of an adolescent girl, caught in the clutches of the systematic persecution of the Jews under Hitler. Don't let the terrible tensions and dramatic details of those two long years of hiding divert attention from this "inside" view of adolescence.

HURLOCK, ELIZABETH. *Adolescent Development*. New York: McGraw-Hill Book Co., 1949. A clear, comprehensive coverage of a topic about which many lay "experts" have innumerable unsound theories. A useful reference book.

JOSSELYN, IRENE M. *The Adolescent and His World*. New York: Family Association of America, 1955. This brief book is chiefly designed for

137

those who have had basic training in psychology and who have professional responsibility for dealing with adolescent persons and their families. Very useful.

LIGON, ERNEST. *Their Future is Now.* New York: The Macmillan Co., 1959. Dr. Ligon draws on thirty years' psychological research on character development as he describes his goal-centered approach to Christian character training, based on the Beatitudes. The book looks in the direction of developing strengths rather than merely correcting weaknesses. Its stress upon bite-sized goals should be of particular value to those working with the hard-to-reach.

ROTH, ARTHUR, M.D. *The Teen Age Years.* Garden City, New York: Doubleday and Co., Inc., 1960. A readable, up-to-date coverage of growth toward physical maturity in teen-age persons, written by the director of one of the first clinics in this country to specialize in teen-age medicine.

WATTENBERG, WILLIAM W. *The Adolescent Years.* New York: Harcourt, Brace and Co., 1955. The value in this book lies more in its breadth than its depth. Interestingly, the closing chapters focus upon adult concerns relating to young people. Each chapter lists useful audiovisual resources as well as readings for further studies.

WITTENBERG, RUDOLPH. *Adolescence and Discipline.* New York: Association Press, 1959. The author is a psychotherapist with a complementary background of experience as a worker with youth groups in New York. He offers here a discerning and lucid view of the nature and dynamics of discipline, for the practical benefit of parents, teachers, and other leaders of young persons.

II. Emotional Problems of Young Persons.

BETTELHEIM, BRUNO. *Love Is Not Enough.* Glencoe, Ill.: The Free Press, 1950. One reviewer's comment on this book was "One of the very few works which describe how an institution can be effective, scientific —and human." Here, in the context of residential work with severely disturbed children, are clues for helping other children live well with themselves and with others.

GALLAGHER, J. ROSWELL, M.D. and HERBERT I. HARRIS, M.D. *Emotional Problems of Adolescents.* New York: Oxford University Press, 1958. This is a simply written discussion of the emotional problems with which adolescent persons are most likely to struggle. The content is nontechnical, but sound psychologically; a helpful resource for persons having special responsibilities for guiding young persons toward maturity.

PEARSON, GERALD H. J. *Emotional Disorders of Children.* New York: W. W. Norton and Co., Inc., 1949. The author speaks of this as a "casework in child psychiatry." As such, it tends to be a bit more technical than some of the other books listed here. The material is amply illustrated and systematically arranged. This is a fine basic resource for a small library focusing upon juvenile development.

REDL, FRITZ and DAVID WINEMAN. *Children Who Hate*. Glencoe, Ill.: The Free Press, 1951. An arresting and perhaps disturbing analysis of intensive efforts to deal with severely disturbed children in a residential clinical setting. One should also read the sequel to this study, *Controls From Within*, which points toward the development of inner control in such children.

REDL, FRITZ and DAVID WINEMAN. *Controls From Within*. Glencoe, Ill.: The Free Press, 1952. Keep in mind that these two books deal with the problems of children whose extreme, aggressive behavior necessitates comprehensive residential programs of treatment. From them, we should gain valuable insights for preventive work with hard-to-reach, aggressive young persons.

III. Juvenile Gangs.

COHEN, ALBERT K. *Delinquent Boys—The Culture of the Gang*. Glencoe, Ill.: The Free Press, 1955. A good grounding in some of the cultural facets of the "delinquent solution" to the problems of adolescent boys.

HANSON, KITTY. *Rebels in the Streets*. Englewood Cliffs, N.J.: Prentice-Hall, Inc., 1964. This is a social worker's review of an assignment with a gang of bad-acting adolescent girls. Though it contains an ample supply of the sensational, the book offers some useful insight into the nature of teenage gang associations. Further, it offers some clues to particular needs which lead a girl to delinquent behavior.

THRASHER, FREDERICK M. *The Gang*. Chicago: University of Chicago Press, 1927. Though this book was written more than a generation ago, its description of the relationships involved in gang associations is still helpful. That some gang behavior patterns have been lately modified in no way diminishes the value of the work.

IV. The Young Offender as a Person.

GRAZIANO, ROCKY. *Somebody Up There Likes Me*. New York: Pocket Books, Inc., 1956. A true story, offering a hard, "inside" picture of a tough kid from the lower East Side of New York. Don't get thrown by the dramatic details; watch rather for what they say about the persons involved.

LINDNER, ROBERT. *Rebel Without a Cause*. New York: Grune and Stratton Medical and Psychology Publishers, 1944. A straight-from-the-shoulder description of the anguish of a young person who, amid his adolescent transitions, is tormented by loneliness and lovelessness and a consequent lack of direction.

VAN WATERS, MIRIAM. *Youth in Conflict*. New York: Republic Publishing Co., 1926. This is a classic purview of some of the arenas of conflict in which delinquent young persons do battle. Dr. Van Waters does this on the basis of long personal experience. She insists that readers and all social workers see those with whom they deal as *persons*. Ample supply of illustrative material.

V. Juvenile Delinquency Taken as a Whole.

AICHORN, AUGUST. *Wayward Youth*. New York: Meridian Books, 1955. This book, first published in Vienna in 1925, is still a valuable contribution to the psychoanalytical understanding of delinquent young people. The work is neither exhaustive nor definitive, but theoretically sound, and based on direct experience.

EISSLER, K. R., Ed. *Searchlights on Delinquency*. New York: International Universities Press, 1949. Fourth Printing, 1958. This is a collection of papers by recognized specialists in analytically oriented approaches to delinquency. A small library in itself, well fortified with bibliographcal material.

FINE, BENJAMIN. *1,000,000 Delinquents*. New York: The World Publishing Co., 1955. This is a newspaper correspondent's perceptive review of the problem of juvenile delinquency in mid-twentieth century America. It is saturated with observations and evaluations by delinquent boys and girls themselves and urges the development of community team efforts for both remedial and preventive action.

FRIEDLANDER, KATE. *Psychoanalytical Approach to Juvenile Delinquency*. London: Routledge and Kegan Paul Ltd., 1947. The author focuses upon those facets of juvenile delinquency to which psychoanalytic findings may be best applied. Further, the book offers suggestions for the use of psychoanalytic insights in the fields of psychology, penology, and social service, in terms of both preventive and remedial therapy.

GLUECK, ELEANOR and SHELDON. *Delinquents in the Making*. New York: Harper & Brothers, Publishers, 1952. A distillation of the longer and more technical report on the Gluecks' ten-year study of 1,000 delinquent boys. Much attention is here turned toward "Paths to Prevention." The reader will be interested in the soon-to-be-published results of tests of the validity of the Gluecks' "Delinquency Prediction" tables.

McCANN, RICHARD V. *Delinquency: Sickness or Sin?* New York: Harper & Brothers, Publishers, 1957. Dr. McCann calls churches concerned about delinquency prevention to a greater appreciation of the role of a person's self image and the models by which he patterns his behavior. The author suggests that we realize that the sickness and sin of the delinquent is *ours*.

TAPPAN, PAUL W. *Juvenile Delinquency*. New York: McGraw-Hill Book Co., Inc., 1949. This book is written to supplement the meager supply of material dealing with the pertinent sociological and legal aspects of juvenile delinquency. Its concern with treatment and prevention is founded upon these joint concerns.

VEDDER, CLYDE, Ed. *The Juvenile Offender*. Garden City, New York: Doubleday and Co., Inc., 1954. A well-documented survey of some problems raised by young offenders. The articles are accompanied by extensive bibliographical material for further study. A very readable resource book.

VI. Toward Church and Community Work with Young Offenders.

BERNSTEIN, SAUL. *Youth on the Streets*. New York: Association Press, 1964. An excellent, up-to-the-moment discussion of current community efforts to reach unrelated street groups. Its chief concern is the widening gap which Mr. Bernstein says is separating "sub-lower class" youth and the respectable adult community. The book covers material often overlooked in casual treatments of the subject.

KENRICK, BRUCE. *Come Out the Wilderness*. New York: Harper & Bros., 1962. The story of the haunting struggle of three young ministers and then of a "visible body of (lay) Christians" to be the Church in the heart of Harlem, New York. A compelling picture of telling ministries with hard-to-reach persons. This is a firsthand story about the now-famous East Harlem Protestant Parish.

KVARACEUS, WILLIAM C. *The Community and the Delinquent*. Yonkers, New York: World Book Company, 1954. This book nicely indicates the wide range of concerns, and, to some extent, the cooperation which is essential to any effective community endeavor to deal with the problems announced by delinquent behavior. One could wish that it would say more about *how* that community cooperation is actually achieved.

McCORKLE, LLOYD, ALBERT ELIAS, and F. LOVELL BIXBY. *The Highfields Story*. New York: Henry Holt and Co., 1958. The report of an adventurous experiment in "guided group treatment" for delinquent boys in New Jersey. The program has since been used in modified form in several parts of the country.

MYERS, C. KILMER. *Light the Dark Streets*. Greenwich, Conn.: The Seabury Press, Inc., 1957. This is the stimulating story of direct, aggressive church approach to hard-to-reach inner city young people. Very helpful, provided the reader does not conclude that the entire responsibility of the Church in this area lies in the establishment of similar dramatic programs.

PALMER, CHARLES E. *The Church and the Exceptional Person*. New York: Abingdon Press, 1961. The chief value of this book is its indication of the urgent need for much more comprehensive treatment of the topics upon which it touches.

ROGERS, CARL R. *Client-Centered Therapy*. Boston: Houghton Mifflin and Co., 1951. The father of non-directive counseling brings together a review of his therapeutic approach, some of its developing applications, and some of its implications for the theoretical understanding of the nature and development of personality.

WEIHOFEN, HENRY. *The Urge to Punish*. New York: Farrar, Straus and Cudahy, 1956. Henry Weihofen received the American Psychiatric Association's fourth annual Isaac Ray Award for "his contribution to the improvement of the relations of law and psychiatry." Note particularly the discussion in the first and last chapters of the overlapping concerns of these two fields.

WILLIAMS, COLIN W. *Where in the World*. New York: National Council of Churches Office of Publication and Distribution, 1963. A provocative discussion of the Christian Mission in the world God so loves that he offers his Son for its salvation. Excellent preparatory reading for those seriously considering continuing ministries with hard-to-reach persons.

Journals and Periodicals

Children. Children's Bureau, U.S. Dept. of Health, Education, and Welfare; Washington, D.C., Publishers. A quarterly presentation of concerns relating to children. It is prepared for the benefit of professional social workers in the field. Good source of information and representative thinking.

Crime and Delinquency. Published by National Conference on Crime and Delinquency, New York. This report concerns itself mostly with philosophies of treatment and issues for long-term social action efforts.

Federal Probation. Published by Administrative Office of U.S. Courts; Washington, D.C. A fine quarterly resource for a brief sampling of current thinking about the work of the courts and related institutions with both juvenile and adult offenders.

International Journal of Religious Education. Published by the Division of Christian Education, National Council of Churches of Christ in the U.S.A. This monthly cooperative church publication frequently deals with particular educative and evangelistic challenges raised by adolescent young people, both within and quite without the church. The treatment is consistently current and sound.

The Journal of Pastoral Care. Published by the Council for Clinical Training and Institute for Pastoral Care, New York. A rather scholarly quarterly publication. Definitely a professional treatment of issues and interpretations of pastoral work and clinical pastoral training. Brief but authoritative material of current significance.

Pastoral Psychology. Pastoral Psychology Press, Great Neck, New York. A monthly magazine mainly designed for ministers, focusing on varying aspects of pastoral care. A very readable treatment of material which is both theologically and psychologically sound and which draws a major portion of its contents from the actual experience of its contributors.

INDEX